Rescued

Ransomed

Restored

BARBARA SAUNDERS LIVINGSTON

Editing by Rachael Van Horn and Sarah Nishimuta

Book Formatting by Jeanie Lemaster

Cover design editing by David Wallace at D. Wallz Studios

ISBN-13: 978-1721836352

ISBN-10: 1721836357

DEDICATION

This book is dedicated first and forever foremost to my Savior and Lord; Jesus. Salvation and Life is found in no other. If not for His willing, brutal sacrificial death on the cross, as well as resurrection I would be lost, imprisoned, tormented, separated from anything good or loving - without hope. Jesus, You are it for me. I love you. I live for you. I will worship You with my last breath.

I also wrote this book for my daughters, Renee', Deanna, and Brook. I am so grateful Father lifted me out of darkness, so I could raise you saved, sober, and in Christ. May my story serve as a heritage, direction, and a warning. If you find yourself lost, lonely, broken, or confused, look to the cross, bow to Jesus. He is always the answer. I love you.

To my grandchildren, Ledger, Preston and Lauren my heart overflows with love and joy for all of you.

To my parents Dean and LaVonne who adopted me, loved me, and raised me. Thank you.

To my grandparents JD and Mollie Shoopman who were always loving and supportive.

To my biological parents, James and Vonda, who brought me into the world and agreed to reunite.

To my biological brothers, John and Robert, I'm so thankful Father led me to you and reunited us. I love you both.

In Loving Memory
My Dad Floyd Dean Saunders
Grandpa JD and Grandma Mollie Shoopman
My biological father James Fenton White, Jr.
My four babies beholding the face of God and running on the playgrounds of Heaven

CONTENTS

ENDORSEMENTS

There was once a woman whom I met in a church nursery hallway. Uncharacteristically I asked her, "What's your story?" That one question would bring her into a 10-year journey. The journey included: a salvation that seemed tested by fire, a personal love story for our Lord Jesus Christ, a deep love for devouring God's Word, hours and hours of counseling, service projects, ministry endeavors, and freedom from the world of perversion and prostitution.

She was a woman who began a journey of victory while facing many "Jericho Valleys". In the valley, she was emotionally beaten, left in the mud, and caught in the snares of human nature and bureaucracy.

This journey thrust her into intense spiritual warfare, tears and frustration and disappointment that seemed to crush the spirit, mind, and body. Yet in all of this, the voice of the Lord was heard and obeyed.

She was told, "Take heart, for one day you will be free and a nurse" because it is all part of His story for her life.

This book confronts the reader with the question of, "What's your story?" But it continues with a bigger question of, what will you do with His story in your life?

May the Lord bless and encourage everyone who reads this book.

Dr. Tony Barros
Pastor and Friend
Chaplain for Oklahoma Wing Civil Air Patrol,
Chaplain for Woodward Police Department
Former Associate Pastor First Baptist Church, Woodward, Oklahoma

I can honestly say that I had never heard of human sex trafficking until I became a state legislator. The thought of someone, especially young children, being subjected to such horrific defilement tore my heart in two, and I wondered how a person could ever overcome such devastating violation.

Then I met Barbara, an actual victim of sex trafficking. Her joy, her zest for life, her hope in the future will inspire you. And you'll soon learn that it is her love for the Lord and her uncompromising devotion to serve Him that have made her "more than a conqueror" in spite of all she has endured in her life.

Her book will enlighten you, inspire you, tear at your heart, and motivate you to want to be "more than a conqueror" too in your own life. *Sally Kern, Oklahoma State Representative, HD 84 2005-2016*

Through the years of serving my country in the military and FBI, I've seen, first hand, lives destroyed as a result of human tragedy, whether self-inflicted or because of circumstances beyond their control. Every day, they battle with burdens such as war, sickness, disease, poverty, crime, addictions, oppression, brutality, and more.

Many of these people drift in and out of churches searching for hope, but never develop a relationship with Jesus Christ, the only one who could free them. They eventually accept their "fate" and settle for a life filled with bitterness and pain.

Thank-you Barbara for being an example of one who has overcome such obstacles through your faith in Jesus Christ. Stay strong, never give up! The world needs to hear your testimony!

Ruth 3:11 "And now my daughter, do not fear, I will do for you all that you ask, for all my fellow townsman know that you are a worthy woman." FBI *Agent, Davis*

My first encounter with Barbara Saunders Livingston was through the bars of a jail cell. It was a brief encounter that would lead to a longtime friendship. Jail ministry is a matter of planting seed and leaving the rest up to God. It was only later that I learned that Barbie had indeed had a spiritual encounter with the Lord.

The next time I saw her and had a chance to visit with her was when I learned that she had been released to a rehabilitation facility and as a new person in Christ was now going by the name of Barbara. Needless to say, it was such a blessing to see the changes that the Lord had made in her life.

I have continued to watch Barbara grow in the Lord, set goals in her life and achieve them. As with all of us there have been ups and downs in her life but she has continued to trust the Lord through it all.

I am so grateful to God, He has allowed me to see what He can accomplish when just a tiny little grain of seed is dropped in fertile soil and then fed and watered by others to grow a wonderful Christian woman.

Sharon Jackson
Gideons International Auxiliary
Faithful witness for Christ in Woodward County Jail for 17 years

BROKEN

Filth layered the gas station bathroom. The smell of stale urine bored into my senses as I dipped the point of the syringe into the toilet water to fill it.

On my knees in front of the toilet bowl, I pushed a stream of water from the syringe into the spoon I had placed on the concrete floor. The meth started dissolving into the liquid. Using the end of my syringe, I crushed the remaining crystal-like rocks. I ripped off a small piece of filter from a cigarette, rolled it up in a ball between my fingers then dropped it down into the thickening solution.

As I watched the cotton absorb and expand, I lowered the point of the needle on top, drew up the dope, then lifted it in vertical view. I thumped the clear cylinder as a few remaining bubbles rushed to the top. I placed the loaded syringe between my teeth and bit the barrel. I used my shirt as a tourniquet twisting it tight around my arm causing my antecubital vein to swell to the surface of my skin. During the process of this repetitive ritual and just before I injected the evil into my bloodstream, I thought to myself, "This is what I do. This is who I am."

A day does not go by when I do not think of those who are lost in the darkness. Because I was one of them.

This is my story. A story of childhood abuse, abandonment, confinement, addiction, sex trafficking and months in jail which exposed me, ultimately, to the one thing which could save me.

I sat and prayed with so many from all walks of life who are addicted to sin, in prisons and jails, institutions, homeless shelters, dope houses, street corners, hospitals, drug and alcohol rehabs.

But I also saw the snares related to self-righteous, religious pew sitting and bondages of all kinds. All precious people who are lonely, confused, trapped, broken, tired, weary, hopeless, empty, and searching.

Since my salvation in a jail cell twenty years ago, I have an insatiable desire to offer others what has been freely given to me. I want others to know there is a way out; but only one way out. I didn't find the one way, I learned He found me. I assure you I did not wake up one day in a jail cell having almost lost my own life including everything worth anything to me and decide to follow Christ.

He pursued me. He called me. He came for me. He found me.

Here, there is freedom. There is love. There is peace. There really is joy. There is hope. There is a purpose and a point to it all. There is One who can RESCUE. One who can RANSOM your life. One who is able to RESTORE us back to His original intent and purpose. His name is JESUS.

Jesus answered, "I am the way and the truth and the life. No one comes to the Father except through me." John 14:6 (NIV)

No two stories are the same. However, as I have traveled and transparently shared what I've walked through and from which I have been delivered, it is apparent there are many, many who can relate in some way.

There is a certain comfort experienced in realizing others have walked through similar circumstances. We simply need to be real and transparent with God and one another.

If by reading this, you receive or take away anything from my story, know what I've been commissioned and sent to tell you, there is hope. All things are possible in Christ. No matter your situation or circumstances, there is hope. Never give up. Turn to Jesus. He will bring you out and through. Victory is in Him.

"They (born-again believers) overcame and triumphed over him (Satan) by the blood of the Lamb (Jesus) and by the word of their testimony; they did not love their lives so much as to shrink from death (Revelation 12:11).

My name is Barbara. I am a Registered Nurse, a mother, a grandmother, a wife and a saved sinner who has been tragically damaged and wonderfully delivered. This is my testimony.

RESCUED

[res-kyood]

verb

1. To free or deliver from
confinement, violence, danger, or evil

2. Law. to liberate or take by
forcible or illegal means from lawful
custody

Source: Dictionary.com

RELINQUISHED

*Though my father and mother forsake me, the
LORD will receive me. Psalm 27:10*

"No reason to be scared. Not to worry. I will take care of us. I'll make sure we are safe. We will sleep on benches if we have to and I will find something for us to eat."

There were times something triggered the need to survive.

At the age of 5 years and 4 months this is what I began explaining to my fourteen-month-old little sister. With an intense, almost primal need to escape and protect us, I somehow managed to lift her up and over the 6-foot backyard fence, causing her to land on the concrete on the other side. I then climbed over the fence myself.

My little sister had been walking for only about 5 months. I held her hand as we walked down our neighborhood street in Bethany, Oklahoma, down a large hill through a public park, across 23rd, a busy four-lane street to a grocery store called Skaggs Alpha Beta (Later Albertsons).

I spotted the manager watching me trying to get food for us, so I left.

I led her back across the street to the school playground where I attended kindergarten at Western Oaks Elementary. I hid her in a huge black tractor tire laying on its side. I can't remember how long we stayed there but the police eventually found us and took us back home. Apparently, an adult called the police after they saw two children in the store and crossing the busy street.

When I was little, I struggled from the effects of what I initially considered abandonment, rejection, being unloved and unwanted.

Mom, Kent (adopted brother), and me (almost 3 years old) at Silver Dollar City for a vacation already planned when my parents received the call from DHS child welfare office informing them they had a little girl who needed a forever home.

I was placed in a foster home and adopted when I was almost three years old. My adoptive parents (from this point forward referred to as Mom and Dad) renamed me Barbie, reasoning my original name Barbara was too big of a name for a little girl.

From the time I can remember I always knew I was adopted. I just could never understand exactly why I was adopted. I figured the very people who brought me into this world, who were supposed to love me and protect me, didn't want me. This and the unknown circumstances surrounding my relinquishment as a baby, set the stage for and birthed certain vulnerabilities within me.

Consequently, I experienced tremendous difficulty truly bonding with my adopted parents and family, or really anyone. I was terrified of being touched and receiving affection, especially from men. I didn't experience feelings I can remember in the early years, except for perhaps fear and soon to follow, shame.

I suspect I had so shut-down emotionally prior to and in the process of my adoption my dad would later report to the "professionals", upon my admission to the first long-term psychiatric institution, he had never seen me cry but once. I was 13-years-old. It was when the topic of my biological parents was discussed officially for the first time.

When someone touched me, I froze. My body became stiff. I was unable to speak. If I were to assign a response or emotion to describe those moments it would be petrified.

There were a couple of occasions my mom mentioned in vague language, yet with a serious as well as a compassionate face, my biological beginnings, "Must have been really bad. Something really bad must have happened," she would say.

My parents' legal representative in Canadian county, Oklahoma did not disclose specifics about my beginnings to my parents at the time of my adoption. It was considered a closed adoption.

My grandma Mollie worked at the Oklahoma State Health Department at the time and as my sealed adoption records came across her desk she did not indulge any curiosity.

From the time I can remember I knew I was adopted. Being adopted in and of itself held no negative connotation, other than wondering what had happened to me to require my adoption. It's just the way it was. I knew nothing different and I don't believe I was treated differently by anyone externally because of it.

Riding my new tricycle at my new forever home in Piedmont, Oklahoma.

At this point, the problem wasn't about what was going on around me. The problem was what was happening within me.

Early on I made no connection between my personality, my behavior, my emotional responses, or lack thereof, and how I processed life and relationships directly to why I was an adopted child. This was suggested later by professionals in the field of psychology - some good, some not so good - and books I read.

I do believe what happened to me before my adoption and the way our spiritual enemy takes advantage of children, the wounded, the weak, and the vulnerable did create a dynamic in my mind and heart requiring nothing less than the blood sacrifice of Christ on the cross to heal me.

It was both my cross and my salvation. It led me to the truth of the Word of God, the powerful work of the Spirit of God, and the love of God flowing through the people of God, who helped to administer healing, redemption, and assisted in bringing me to salvation, including the process of transformation.

There was value in learning some tools and basic truths related to human nature. But my transformation was of the spirit and identity.

I now know my adopted parents wanted me and did the best they knew to love and raise me as their own. They provided a very nice, clean home, clothing, education, work ethic, piano lessons and the values, honesty and integrity.

However, my fear of and inability to receive physical touch or love without being terrified, scarred me so deeply. I did not possess the understanding or skills to process, communicate, or remember the events, changes, and emotions in my young life. My pain and fear regarding those relationships was transferred onto my adopted family.

The enemy literally stole some parts of my childhood from me. Those perceptions so owned me they colored my view of my own worth and safety within my family.

I learned much later when trauma and abuse happen either a fight-or-flight or dissociative response occurs. I seemed to mostly dissociate but there were occasions I would attempt to take flight. I didn't learn to fight until years later. And even more years after to fight in a healthy way.

"IT IS IMPORTANT TO REMEMBER THAT TRAUMA RESPONSE CAN BE TRIGGERED BY ANYTHING AN ABUSE VICTIM ASSOCIATES WITH HER ABUSE, AND WHAT WE MAY PERCEIVE AS HARMLESS, SHE MIGHT PERCEIVE AS A GENERALIZED THREAT. JUST A SIMPLE REMINDER OF A PAST ABUSIVE INCIDENT CAN HURL A YOUNG GIRL DOWN THE DESTRUCTIVE CYCLE OF COMPLETELY DISCONNECTING AND DISENGAGING FROM WHAT IS GOING ON AROUND HER. THIS STRANGE BEHAVIOR IS OFTEN MISUNDERSTOOD BY CARETAKERS, WHO OBSERVE ONLY THE SURFACE PROBLEMS OF BAD ATTITUDE OR DEFIANT BEHAVIOR INSTEAD OF THE DEEPER CAUSE UNDERNEATH. SADLY, GIRLS WHO HAVE BEEN ABUSED OFTEN DO NOT SHOW OUTWARD SIGNS OF WHAT IS GOING ON PSYCHOLOGICALLY UNTIL THEY BEGIN EXHIBITING SELF-SOOTHING BEHAVIORS SUCH AS CUTTING THEMSELVES OR TURNING TO DRUG ABUSE.

GENERALIZED REMINDERS CAN TRIGGER THESE RESPONSES, AND BECAUSE THE VICTIM OF ABUSE IS IN A CONSTANT STATE OF SENSITIVITY TO THESE THREATS, SHE CAN JUMP FROM VAGUE APPREHENSION TO A STATE OF CRIPPLING FEAR WITHIN SECONDS AND MAY ASSESS RISK LIKE A CHILD AND RESPOND TO HARMLESS ACTIONS OF AUTHORITY AS IF THAT PERSON INTENDS TO DO HER HARM. THIS REACTION IS OFTEN SEEN IN A CONDITION KNOWN AS POST-TRAUMATIC STRESS DISORDER, OR PTSD. ORDINARY SIGHTS AND SOUNDS THAT NEVER SEEMED THREATENING BEFORE CAN TRIGGER A FIGHT-OR-FLIGHT RESPONSE. (2012, THE WHITE UMBRELLA, WELLSPRING LIVING)

I stole my parent's jewelry from their bedroom. My mom would find the stash in my shoes at the bottom of my closet. I also hid food. I remember cutting my face out of a family picture.

These, I would learn later, are behaviors which foster or adopted children exhibit sometimes, having faced and endured neglect, abuse, and abandonment.

In the book "The White Umbrella" by Mary Frances Bowley it states,

"Environmental cues can also change the course in the developing brain by redefining what is considered "normal." Experiences provide templates in the brain that determine how life is interpreted, as well as what makes a person laugh, cry, love, hate, remember events, create beliefs. It also controls what each person views as "safe." These environmental cues teach children what they can trust and what they should fear.

Because the brain is so formative and vulnerable in these early years, childhood abuse influences how a person makes decisions and assesses risk later in life."

These deficits while I was a child caused me to see relationships, especially with my adopted parents, through very wounded and broken lenses. I simply struggled to believe my parents loved and sincerely wanted me.

When I was in the 4th grade, about 9-years-old returning from Christmas break, the class was given an assignment. We were asked to write or tell about something special which happened while we were out of school during the break.

I chose to give a verbal report. My teacher called my mom, had her come to the school, and gave her an overview of the report I shared. She explained to my mom how I discussed with the class how great my biological parents were and how I didn't understand how or why my dad and mom kept me from living with them.

The teacher notified the district psychologist who came and talked with me a few times. The teacher knew, and the psychologist was made aware I was adopted and had no contact with my biological parents. I readily admitted I made the story up.

They concluded to Mom I just wanted to try and impress my peers which was quite common with this age group and this event was considered isolated due to "nothing out of the ordinary" happening between the kindergarten episode with my sister and this fantasy report. At least I thought so till junior high.

I learned later it is not uncommon occurrence for adopted children, at some point, to fantasize about their biological life, parents, and beginnings. However, what I remember from this event isn't the made-up story to fit an assignment, Mom being called to the school, or the meetings with a psychologist but rather what I now know to be the trace and face of shame. Shame, meaning not just what I say or do as being bad and wrong, but there being something wrong with who I am.

I had really very little insight or awareness of anything on a deeper level other than survival.

On the face of it, I adapted well enough. I did well in school and like most moms, my mom would say everything was going well enough at the time. Despite these below-the-surface deficits birthed from traumatic events and abuse I would learn about much later, I transitioned and made a few friends along the way.

There were good moments and memories growing up. I grew up with my brother who was five years older than me and adopted prior to my adoption. My little sister, who my mom and dad gave birth to after my adoption, was also important to me. I remember being closest to her. She and I played together a lot.

Me and my little sister Lanetta at holiday dinner in 2017

I loved them all the best way I understood how to love and was capable of at this time.

Between the ages of 12 to 13, questions began to surface within me surrounding how I came to be adopted. What really happened to me? Why wasn't I with my biological parents? What did all this mean about my worth? Up until this time, I had not yet begun to process the reality of why I was adopted; not really.

As a result, I was exposed to negative terms such as abandonment, unwanted and rejected.

I conflated the word adoption to mean all those things. It was all coming at a time during what I would consider normal development for my age and the search for one's identity, fitting-in with friends at school, and the soon to come rebellion often associated with what some professionals call self-actualization. It all began to take its toll on me.

13

REBELLION

*For rebellion is as the sin of witchcraft, and
stubbornness is as iniquity and idolatry."*

1 Samuel 15:23

As a young teen and with a buried spirit of rejection owning me
on the one hand and a new spirit of rebellion entering on the other,
my decisions and the events which followed during these next years
changed my life in devastating ways.

At the young age of 13, I was exposed to a woman who was into
witchcraft.

However, it's important to note during this time, my parents
were doing all they could to provide me with a relatively stable life. I
was protected and provided for. I had good friends I hung out with.
We had fun and laughed. I made good grades, was in pep club, went
to basketball and football games. I played basketball and softball.

In elementary school I had a friend named Katie. We spent the night at each other's houses, met at the end of the street on our bikes, and enjoyed family vacations together.

My elementary school friend, Katie and I having lunch years later.

I enjoyed helping my mom around the house, outside with chores and playing with my little sister. Our family built a cabin together at Cedar Lake in Hinton, Oklahoma where we would take summer vacations to swim and fish in the lake.

I also sang in choir, played piano and performed in recitals. My parents offered me the option of taking gymnastic lessons or piano lessons. No brainer! I was so excited by the idea of playing a piano!

I took lessons from a woman named Bessie, just down the road for approximately five years. I was required to practice almost daily for thirty-minute increments. As relatively stable and as well as I had seemed to adjust, there was a part of me repressed.

The piano opened a door to my expression.

My Piano

When I would sit down to play piano, it would soothe a deep place inside. It was something I practiced regularly and enjoyed. It was a kind of escape.

One song, particularly, touched this spot and has stayed with me all these years. There was a bird flying on the front page of the piece called "Flying Free". Even at a young age the title, the picture of the bird in flight and the words comforted the broken little girl inside me.

This called to the free, whole and healed child of God I would one day become.

Yet, this reality was still so far off.

FLYING FREE- WORDS AND MUSIC BY DON BESIG

THERE IS A PLACE I CALL MY OWN

WHERE I CAN STAND BY THE SEA

AND LOOK BEYOND THE THINGS I'VE KNOWN

AND DREAM THAT I MIGHT BE FREE

LIKE A BIRD ABOVE THE TREES

GLIDING GENTLY ON THE BREEZE

I WISH THAT ALL MY LIFE I'D BE

WITHOUT A CARE AND FLYING FREE

BUT LIFE IS NOT A DISTANT SKY

WITHOUT A CLOUD, WITHOUT RAIN

AND I CAN NEVER HOPE THAT I

CAN TRAVEL ON WITHOUT PAIN

TIME GOES SWIFTLY ON IT'S WAY

ALL TOO SOON WE'VE LOST TODAY

I CANNOT WAIT FOR SKIES OF BLUE

OR DREAM SO LONG

THAT LIFE IS THROUGH

SO LIFE'S A SONG THAT I MUST SING

A GIFT OF LOVE THAT I MUST SHARE

AND WHEN I SEE THE JOY IT BRINGS,

MY SPIRITS SOAR THROUGH THE AIR

LIKE THAT BIRD UP IN THE SKY

LIFE HAS TAUGHT ME HOW TO FLY

FOR NOW I KNOW WHAT I CAN BE

AND NOW MY HEART IS FLYING FREE

In junior high my best friend was Mindi. We laughed about everything, and we couldn't care less about what people thought of us. Time with Mindi was a snap shot for fun times and a taste of some happiness.

My best friend Mindi in junior high.

Mindi's family attended a Church of Christ and they took me with them a few times. I was beginning to get close to hearing the truth. I never forgot this verse I learned at Mindi's church.

> *And now these three remain: faith, hope, and*
> *love. But the greatest of these is love.*
> *1 Corinthians 13:13*

I also had a boyfriend who played football. Kyle was a nice guy who treated me kindly. His family was friendly and welcomed me. He took me to his church, Council Road Baptist church, a couple times as well. Kyle and his family were a window to something good.

Advancing from elementary to junior high at Western Oaks, required we change buildings and rotate classrooms. Other schools combined with ours which meant new faces.

There was a new guy who had come from New York. His hair, his accent, his attitude was all different. He wore a black leather jacket, combat boots and had an earring. He wore chains, weird jewelry and smoked cigarettes.

He began talking to me, showing interest and giving me attention. He started coming to my house and I would visit with him on the cement wall outside. He began sharing his cigarettes with me. Then one day he kissed me.

The relationship I had with my mom grew increasingly strained and distant. She set rules and boundaries in areas of my life like make-up, clothes, curfew, friends, school, etc. There was a lot of arguing. I began thinking she was against me and even hated me. I continued to do what my new boyfriend was wanting and asking me to do. I began making choices which would continue to drive a wedge between my parents and me.

I now realize we are responsible for our own choices. However, I was not aware of the reason I was making the decisions I was.

My mom would later describe this time by saying, "She went to bed a little girl and woke up a woman". She said I changed dramatically and devastatingly overnight.

I began trying to dress like him and changing my look to match his style - darker clothes, darker make-up. I began listening to his music, considered "new wave". I didn't think it was a big deal at the time. I didn't realize the change occurring in and around me. I certainly didn't understand it because I was kind of naive. I was becoming blind and deceived.

Regarding this year of my life and the events happening, my best friend Mindi recently shared this:

> "Barbie seemed to change a little. We began to spend less time together. Then it seemed like all of a sudden Barbie was just gone. I didn't know what happened. I just remember feeling very confused and sad MY Barbie was gone.
>
> I had no way of knowing the horror my sweet friend's life had turned into. I thought about her very often over the next 20 years. There was just a little ache in my heart where she had always been."

I do not know, nor can I explain what attracted me to him exactly. Perhaps the attention? Perhaps it was the fact it was new, strange and intriguing? It seems a force had appeared in my life which was stronger than the other things influencing my choices and daily life up to this point.

This did not occur to me, nor did I know how to say "no" or set and establish my own boundaries. I didn't have the knowledge or the tools to stand against what was coming for me.

Then one day he invited me over to his house after school. We walked there, only a couple miles from my home. He introduced me to his mom, who had bright white, spiked hair and wore a floor-length, silky black dress. She was speaking either in another language or with a very thick Italian accent. He had a quick conversation with her and then led me to his bedroom.

I sat down on the edge of the bed in his room. I remember at some point he lit what I now know to be a joint, demonstrated how to hit it, then handed it to me. I did what he did, and we smoked the rest of it. I remember laughing a lot. Then he pushed me down on his bed, got on top of me and had intercourse.

It was over quickly. He got up, put his pants back on, briefly went out of the room and came back with his mother who stepped in looked around, communicated something to him, then left the room. To the best of my knowledge my virginity was now gone.

I fell asleep at his home, woke up, cut my hair off and shaved one side of my head.

Heavy, depressing thoughts began to come over me. Thoughts which said I couldn't go home, my parents were against me. From there, the quality of my thoughts, choices, and life continued to decline immediately. It was the last time I remember ever seeing or talking to either of them.

My mom later shared with me she came to his house looking for me. His mom answered the door and intently informed my mom, "I am a witch. I have your daughter. You will never get her back". My parents called the police, who did end up taking me back home.

My mom would later say this was the first time in her life she had faced what she describes as "evil". It frightened her for me.

I stepped out of the back seat of the police car and walked into the house. My mom was very emotional after seeing my hair. I remember sitting on the couch in the living room and my dad began calmly asking me questions to which I didn't have the answers.

I began to cry. This is the conversation in which he asked me about my biological parents. It was the conversation which he would soon tell the institution, was the only time he had seen me cry.

It seems the real extent of my damage from my first three years had finally surfaced.

For whatever reason it was at this time my eyes were opened to the reality something had to have happened to me to have been adopted. I concluded my biological parents didn't want me and the things happening to me now, added to the conclusion it may've been because there was something wrong with me. Perhaps my suspicions were correct; I wasn't lovable. Perhaps I was evil. Perhaps something so horrific happened to me it would be shameful to even mention.

My sense of not being lovable was consuming me.

I began having overwhelming thoughts of suicide, thinking it was the only way out of this situation. I went upstairs, locked the bathroom door and swallowed pills out of the cabinet, not really wanting to die at this point, but desperately wanting something to change.

My next memory is waking up on the edge of a bed in a hospital.

INSTITUTIONALIZED

For the wages of sin is death... Romans 6:23

Sitting on the edge of the hospital bed I was extremely exhausted. My mom was explaining the situation to me about why I was there.

"You need help," she said. "It's why we are doing this."

My prevailing, recurring thought was, I now wouldn't be able to finish school and graduate.

The thought concerned me greatly and I began expressing it to my mom, who insisted I needed professional help more than I needed to graduate. Looking back now, I understand how she saw my situation.

My decisions, influenced by rejection and rebellion, were the foundation of my institutionalization.

But at the time, in my damaged mind, the actions of my parents seemed to support my sense of self-doubt. They were putting me away from them just like my birth parents had.

Over the next two years, I was in a series of five mental institutions. When one place said they could no longer help me or I would run from a facility – AWOL, or absent without leave, they liked to call it - they would just send me to another place.

Despite good intentions, the institutions reinforced and solidified in my mind there was something wrong with me and I was not wanted or loved. Not only by my biological parents, but also by my adopted parents and family, as well.

My mom and I have had many conversations over the years pertaining to this time in our lives and the manner in which we all responded. I get it now. They were listening to the professionals. They were scared. All they could see was they didn't want me to die.

However, relinquishment after relinquishment of me to someone or something else, communicated to me I was hopeless and helpless, and there was something so wrong with me, even the psychiatrists, psychologists or counselors could not fix it.

I truly believed these destructive messages communicated to me, and I took on this damaging identity very strongly.

There were some medical/clinical terms I was labeled with; depression, dysthymic disorder, dissociative disorder, attachment disorder, addiction, etc. I understand my real diagnosis today is as everyone who has ever lived, who is alive now, or who will ever live.

The Bible calls it sin.

For ALL have sinned and have fallen short of the glory of God. Romans 3:23

I was in jail when I first read this verse. It set me free from my self-absorbed idea there was something so terribly wrong with me which made me worse than everyone else. "All", means everyone.

I understand today, something I was completely oblivious of then; there are spiritual forces of wickedness, and evil principalities and powers feeding on my weakness.

We are all born under the influence of these worldly, demonic suggestions. We are all born into sin.

Not only had I been set up by my biological parents' sin, abuse and neglect, but now through my choice of rebellion against my parents, being subjected to witchcraft, fornication and drug use, it set in motion demonic activity in and around me.

The darkness exploited an open door to my life and body.

The first month of hospitalization in the psychiatric ward at Mercy hospital utilized all the insurance my parents had. Needless to say, it is very expensive to institutionalize someone. My only memory there was visiting with staff a few times and making homemade pizza.

After I was discharged from my first stop, there was a brief time back at home before my dad drove me to my second lock-up facility, Meadowlake Hospital in Enid, Oklahoma. This was a more long-term juvenile institution.

In my mind my mom was influencing the decisions to send me away and I needed more "help".

My feelings of abandonment and rejection were slowly turning to anger. I didn't know what I needed but I was convinced I didn't need to be locked up again. But it didn't matter what I thought.

I walked out of the house with my dad and I saw my mother there standing by our Mercedes, looking sad. I couldn't believe it.

It was a long, mostly silent drive to Meadowlake with my dad. My mom stayed home.

We parked in front of a building with large glass doors. It was like a business office. We were led down the hall. I just stood there. My dad spoke with the people who worked there, and I will never forget the sinking feeling in my chest when he left me there.

He left me there.

MEADOWLAKE HOSPITAL

For the next approximately nine months, Meadowlake Hospital was my home.

Rejection was now my identity. Anger was my only defense and running my survival.

During treatment my parents put me back into the state's custody, which required I go before a judge once a month in Oklahoma City. During the drive from Enid to the City in the facilities van, I would daydream the judge or my mom would say I could go home.

Time and time again my hopes were crushed by an extension. I was considered TITLE 19: IN NEED OF TREATMENT.

This legal process was the avenue my parents would take for assistance and insurance in paying for the expensive treatment I was receiving. But I couldn't understand it. I was just a kid.

These court dates and appearances only reinforced my belief my mom didn't want me and there was something wrong with me. I was in devastating pain. I continued to think death was the only way out.

In addition, I was exposed to many new and difficult things while I was there like the children with a wide variety of behaviors; many on medications caused them to act strangely and desperately.

One boy had beat himself in the head and against things so hard and frequently he had what they called "cauliflower ear". His entire face and head, especially his ears were extremely red, swollen, basically deformed.

The sight of this was shocking. I was sometimes standing next to him in single file line waiting for the locked double doors to open on our way to a daily activity.

Another young boy was so heavily medicated, and the other in-patients made fun of him saying he did the "Thorazine shuffle". He could barely lift his feet when he walked. He drooled all the time and nodded out while we were eating or in a group session. When he ate he got it all over himself. It was sad for me to see.

I spent brief sessions with a psychiatrist, Dr. Feldman, daily. He would ask me how I felt over and over. I didn't know. I didn't know how to express those feelings even if I had known what they were. It was 1987-88.

We basically stared at one another, or I looked at the wall or at the floor while he wrote some things down on his papers.

These sessions were of no comfort or help to me. The psychiatrist had braces on his teeth and, despite the fact he seemed very gentle and kind, had a hard time smiling due to the braces. He wore plaid pastel-colored polo style shirts tucked into tan pants, and penny loafer type shoes.

Staring at the floor while following him off the unit and back before and after sessions, I noticed his pants being too long as he stepped on the back hem leaving a crease and his shirt being a size too large, the cuffs going past his wrists. I observed his small hands as he would always write things on paper in a folder while I sat across from him, glancing up sometimes and smiling at me, awkwardly.

An intervention I realized later to be beneficial was when I was taken into a room with a small table. A sheet of paper was placed in front of me which had many faces on it. The faces had different expressions; much like what we call emoji's today.

The lady taught me what feelings are and how to identify them. She helped me to associate the facial expression with the name of a feeling. It was a very basic practical visual which introduced and created an opening to a few slats of my blinds covering the window into common, expected human emotions. It was an awareness I didn't have before.

There were various therapies and tests. Art therapy, music therapy, individual therapy, group therapy. We also lifted weights, received massage therapy, and played various sports including volleyball in the gym. I went to school at the institution and did my work there with a teacher in a small classroom.

These things helped me survive in the place. But otherwise, there was no point I could see.

I underwent intelligence tests and tests for psychiatric evaluations. One test included ink blots which I later learned is called the Rorschach test. I would look at them for a moment then select the appropriate response(s). Psychologists use this test to examine the personality characteristics and emotional functioning of their patients. The results were never explained to me.

I was also exposed to what they called biofeedback.

A short, stalky man with a mustache and full beard led me to a small room with a computer and sat me in a comfortable reclining chair.

He began attaching electrodes to my skin and body. Finger sensors were also applied. These electrodes/sensors sent signals to a monitor which displayed a sound, flash of light or image represented my heart and breathing rate, blood pressure, skin temperature, sweating or muscle activity, and brain waves. These things are altered when a person is under stress.

He led me through deep breathing, progressive muscle relaxation--alternately tightening and then relaxing different muscle groups, guided imagery, concentrating on a specific image (such as the color and texture of an orange) to focus your mind and make you feel more relaxed, and meditation. The primary image I created was to fall through clouds and land in chocolate pudding.

Years later I renounced involvement in this exercise, because this exercise also has spiritual implications and can be an open door for demons to enter.

I believe, after going through these exercises, God never bypasses the mind to change behavior, but to take every thought captive and make it obedient to Christ.

Do not conform to the pattern of this world but be transformed by the renewing of your mind. Then you will be able to test and approve what God's will is—his good, pleasing and perfect will.
Roman 12: 1-2

He develops our ability to own our choices through the responsibility of free will and our work toward renewing our mind with the Word of God.

The Passion Translation puts it like this:

We can demolish every deceptive fantasy that opposes God and break through every arrogant attitude that is raised up in defiance of the true knowledge of God. We capture, like prisoners of war, every thought and insist that it bow in obedience to the Anointed One.
2 Corinthians 10:5 (TPT)

Again, well-meaning interventions designed to "help", exposed me to yet another entry for the enemy to gain ground into my life forming an identity contrary to God's plans and will for me.

My realizations later, when I discovered who I am as a whole person in Christ, are what delivered me from these fragments of myself which my institutionalization emboldened.

During and after these sessions I was different. I was led into a hypnotic state during those moments of guided imagery and attempts at physiological and mental manipulation. It proved to be a bit more than relaxation exercises.

The psychiatrist began asking me leading questions about my memories before I was adopted, and questions about my biological parents. I maintained I had no specific recollection.

I froze. My body stiffened, like I was trapped almost as if I literally could not speak, feel, or even move. There was not enough time, skills, reciprocating patience, understanding, or gentleness from anyone to allow me to find my way or learn to find the words to speak my truth to the surface.

After many months of being locked up and having nothing to say, I began to shake my head in agreement with what he would suggest, hoping he would say I could go home. It was as if they had to identify something wrong with me, so they could address it and "treat" it before they could release me.

One day in the hall, on the way to being taken to the therapy of the day, I saw my parents coming out of the psychiatrist's room. They had sad, serious looks on their faces, but no one said anything to me. Much later I was told my dad was asked some questions in response to suggestions I made in therapy eluding to my possibly being abused by a man.

Was their suspicion, it could be my adopted dad? When I finally learned about this I was incredulous.

My adopted dad was only good, loving, and kind to me. He was never abusive, only calm. He provided for our family and loved us. This was very difficult to hear and there was no amount of truth to this. I never consciously accused or made allegations of this nature about my adopted dad.

However, there are still lingering questions about what happened to me at the hands of my biological parents.

But this incident at Meadowlake added to my estrangement and confusion and closed a door on any work which could have been helpful at the time.

I was already hurt and angry my parents dropped me off and left me at the institution for so long. At the time I already believed I was a bad, evil person and so difficult to love. Now, the people who I know were trying to care for me, were also suffering from what they thought I was saying.

I attribute this to the type of treatment they were putting me through and possibly what had happened to me as a baby prior to adoption. But the "professionals" never discovered this and, because of it, missed the most obvious signs about how to help me. Instead, they helped injure my dad.

To this day, I hold no recollection or memory of the abuse I learned, much later, indeed did take place at the hands of my biological parents prior to adoption.

I only learned this because, in 1996, I had an attorney get my treatment records and then fought hard later to receive my adoption records.

But at the time, I was still stuck in Meadowlake and now, after seeing the looks on the faces of my parents after the secretive meeting, I was convinced the world was against me.

So, I continued to experience torment and suicidal thoughts. I managed to get ahold of a sewing needle. I self-mutilated with it in my bathroom. I sat on the toilet and repeatedly stuck the inside of my wrist. I found some sense of control by watching the blood appear.

As I write this portion of my story, Isaiah 53:4 comes to mind:

Surely, he took up our pain and bore our suffering, yet we considered Him punished by God, stricken by Him and afflicted. But He was pierced for our transgressions.

Later, I heard it said people who do this are suffering emotionally and mentally. They do it to somehow relieve the mental and emotional pain through temporary physical pain. It was like a release of some sort...transfer of focus.

My sense of imprisonment, isolation, restriction, rejection, and abandonment weighed on me each day. My soul was crying out for grace, love, and mercy. But I didn't know how to find it.

I didn't see a way out of the institution. I thought my prison was the institution. So, my focus was on how to free myself from it. Time passed, weeks turned to months. I still had no real answers as to why I was there or what was 'wrong' with me.

I called home occasionally on a unit phone which was in the dayroom. I spoke to my mom and she remained firm I needed to be there. Each time I was re-wounded when I spoke with her. All I really wanted to hear was when I could leave and go home.

This did not happen.

I was spiraling. The rejection and frustration I was experiencing peaked and I flew into fits of rage. There were triggers immediately prior to these episodes, but it always ended in a "code green" being announced over the intercom system.

One time, after I had talked to my mom on the phone, I began throwing chairs, screaming, cussing and acting out this immense and growing rage.

In a matter of seconds, grown men and women would approach me aggressively, wrestle me down to the ground with multiple adults grabbing ahold of each of my arms, legs, waist, and head. I did not ever go willingly or easily!

On one of these occasions, staff grabbed me so tightly I had red blotches and petechiae all over my chest, neck, and face the next day. I fought them as hard as I could. I screamed obscenities as they restrained me and carried me through the locked doors to what they called seclusion.

The room was small and cell-like, and I was strapped down in a five-point restraint on a table. I fought for a while, jerking and flexing to break free, but eventually would calm down with a sense of defeat. Lacking any awareness of time, I don't know how long I stayed in the position. I was always placed on room restriction for a certain amount of days after - further punishment. Sometimes it was 48 hours, sometimes 72 or 96 hours.

As violent and restrictive as it was, I experienced a certain kind of relief and release after those episodes. Whether it was a release from anger, being provoked into finally expressing myself, or release from pure boredom I'm not certain, but probably a combination of each.

After going off one time and while on room restriction afterward, my psychiatrist came to my room and handed me a book called, "The Road Less Traveled" by M. Scott Peck, MD. I opened it up and recall reading only the first sentence, "Life is difficult."

Indeed.

There was another girl on the unit who seemed annoying to me for some reason. I can't understand my actions at the time. I kept hearing an inner voice pressing me to go beat her up. I resisted and resisted but it was like it just kept encouraging me to go do it for no precise reason. It was the same pressure to "go off" in anger and rage which led me to go into this girl's room while she was resting on her bed and begin throwing punches at her. I beat and beat on her with my fists.

I feel horrible about this and do not exactly understand why or how I could have done this, other than the spirit of rejection I was operating in at the time felt scared and/or threatened by this girl. But now, with a more spiritual lens from which to understand it, I remember witnessing the intense rejection she was suffering within the culture of our hospital environment.

She was me and I hated her.

John 19:1 - Then Pilot ordered Jesus to be brutally beaten with a whip of leather straps embedded with metal.

One day when they let us outside in the courtyard, I decided to run. I went for it and climbed the wall and ran through the park, into a neighborhood. I went up to a home and asked to use the phone. I don't remember much about the attempt, other than I ended up back at the facility with more restrictions and precautions.

My mom came and took me on a 'pass' one day. We had a good enough day together. I had grown several inches in height and gained a lot of weight. I was apparently at the age of a growth spurt. But I also attributed the weight gain to three large meals a day and not a lot of physical activity. The clothes I brought with me to the hospital hardly fit anymore. On pass, my mom bought me a few new clothing items.

When it came time to go back, I began to get apprehensive. She pulled into a gas station and went in the store. While she was in there all I could think of was how I did not want to go back to the ward. I thought, I better move quickly, or I'll miss my chance for freedom.

I got out of the car, ran over and hid behind a dumpster. My mom came out, looked around, called my name, then eventually got in her car and she left. I went to the mall in the town.

I don't remember the events following. I did end up back at the hospital, only this time it wasn't for too long. Arrangements were made to transfer me to another long-term juvenile inpatient facility. They could no longer help me there, they said.

The next facility was in northeastern Oklahoma, called Shadow Mountain in Tulsa. When you think about the redundancy and monotony of life in an institution, any change was a relief. But, in reality, it was a waste of everyone's time.

SHADOW MOUNTAIN HOSPITAL-

My time here was divided between the hospital unit and the drug and alcohol recovery unit. I began on the hospital unit. It was basically an inpatient juvenile psych ward - lock down.

I had private sessions with a psychiatrist, much like Meadowlake, but there were fewer patients. I was only here a few months.

It wasn't as structured as Enid and I had lots of free time, which I used to play the Nintendo and managed to get to the end of a game of Mario Brothers. We had cook-outs and the staff seemed kind.

But the beast inside was still alive and well, and even more cloaked. I was then transferred to the Drug and Alcohol unit of the same campus. It was a mystery to me. I had only smoked one joint and drank alcohol one time up to this date. Hardly criteria for considering someone an addict or an alcoholic.

However, I was glad to be out of a locked mental hospital and onto something new and different. On the hospital unit they had taken me out to walk around the larger campus.

I saw people out and able to walk around, able to breath fresh air! Some of them were carrying a few books in their hand everywhere they went. I soon learned those books were what they called the "Big Book of Alcoholics Anonymous", "Step Book" and "Narcotics Anonymous".

The people on this unit were mostly adults. Maybe one other teenager was a part of them, but I was the youngest. I think I was 14-years-old. I just don't remember my 15th birthday. I was introduced to AA and NA meetings here.

They all admitted they were addicts or alcoholics and responded with heartfelt details about their recovery and experiences. I did not want to admit I was either one because I didn't believe I was and had not drank alcohol or done drugs to the degree the people there said they had.

Again, the confusion for me continued not understanding what was wrong with me or why I was there.

Eventually, I was permitted to attend what they called an 'outside meeting'. It was an Alcoholics Anonymous speaker's meeting. Again, I saw this as my opportunity to run. And ran I did. I walked out of the meeting, across the street and hid in some bushes for a very long time.

Through the leaves of the bushes, I watched cars pass by and everyone depart the meeting. A police car drove by and shined a bright light my way. I remained still behind the bushes pleading to myself, "Please don't find me. I don't want to go back there. I don't want to be locked up".

After what seemed like hours, the sun began to set so I finally crawled out and began walking down the street. I knew nothing of the Tulsa area but had heard of a club in the city named the "Beat Club". Since it was the only place I knew of, I informed the man who picked me up, after sticking my thumb out on the main road to hitchhike, he could just drop me off there. He said he knew where it was, took me there, and dropped me off.

I entered the dance club. I had learned about this place from other teenagers at Shadow Mountain. Loud music, colored lights, and lots of people.

I met two guys while there. One was eighteen and the other around sixteen-years-old. They decided they were going to take a ride. I left with them. They had beer in the vehicle. This is now the second time I drank beer. I proceeded to get very drunk on very little, very quickly. I blacked out – fuzzy, in and out of consciousness.

I came to at one point and was leaning over the car seemingly parked in a field. They were in the process of raping me. There wasn't anything I could do about it because I was so intoxicated.

I ended up with one of the two guys, in his home and in his bed the next day. I stayed there with his family for weeks, may have been even months, in a trailer park not knowing where else to go.

I explained to them where I had been, and I had run from the institution. He lived there with his mom and little brother. He left, never to be seen by me again. His mom allowed me to stay there and every day I watched MTV most of the day. I went to a prison with them to visit their father on a visiting day.

My plan was to get into school there. I was still stuck in this place I was at way back when I was placed into my first institution – My top concern was, I must graduate!

I was also in a survival kind of mentality. Ironically, I thought I was better off living with the man who raped me than in the hospital. In fact, I didn't think of it as being raped, rather the price I had to pay.

The wages of sin is death but the Gift of God is
eternal life through Christ Jesus our Lord.
Romans 6:23

Before I was able to follow through with those grandiose ideas, someone, I assumed it was the younger brother living with us, called the police and told them I was at their home.

The police came. I hid underneath the bed. They dragged me out from underneath the bed by my hair. They took me into the station and questioned me.

I don't remember what I told them, if anything. I sat in a room there for a long time.

My mom explained later, in truth, my dad traced me through a phone number after I made a long distance, collect call to my grandparents. My dad had immediately gone to the local police department and reported my whereabouts.

Apparently, the police then came to the address and talked to me, but Mom says, I convinced them I was someone else.

Much of this I have no memory of. But my mom has helped fill in some details. She went on to say my dad then went to the sheriff's department and they took me out of the house.

After quite some time the police drove me back to the Oklahoma City area. They told me they were taking me back to Bethany. I was extremely relieved to be leaving there and the area. I didn't want to be locked up anymore.

I didn't want to be put into anymore institutions, facilities, or programs.

Yet, I knew where I was being taken. Yet another place. But, it was closer to home. In fact, Bethany Pavilion, where they were taking me, was right down the street from where all this began.

BETHANY PAVILION

By this time, however, my parents had moved to Edmond, another suburb of the city.

I experienced some comfort and sadness knowing I was right there where the hospitalization and institutionalization began. I felt I had come full circle but was the worse for it.

Well over a year had passed. I missed my home. I missed the life I had then, which was to be no more. The chance of "normalcy" was a very distant fleeting daydream, like the flash of a white-tailed deer in the woods. Was it ever really there?

They checked me into this place.

I had a new psychiatrist by the name of Dr. Gilbert. He was a short man. He seemed like a nice man. He talked to me kindly. He listened.

He put me on some type of medication. I began to perceive with this Doctor, there was a small hope he would see I had no real serious diagnosable mental illness. I hope he would let me go home.

During one of the sessions, he let me out of the facility on the playground to talk. I told him I had lived just right up the street and around the corner before all the problems began. He then led us on a walk together away from the facility.

I appreciate even with my history of running, he invested in me and risked taking me out of the facility. We walked up Glade Avenue, then down 19th street and stood in front of the home I grew up in.

Standing there looking at a two-story, white, colonial style home, with the nice yard and the oak tree and monkey grass, feelings of sadness, being violated, and stolen from, surfaced and washed over me. However, this walk he took with me to my former home helped me. It comforted me. I appreciated him for his consideration.

Relatively speaking, it was a fairly calm stay at this place.

I was beginning to think there was maybe some hope I could go home. In fact, one day they called my parents in a room. We all sat there together. The doctor explained some things to them and then announced I was going to get to go home!

It was if I had been wandering in a dry, weary, scary land - in darkness. Relief enveloped me.

I wept.

It was the third time I cried since my adoption. But these were tears of relief. Those were the very words I had been waiting to hear the entire time in these institutions. It had been almost two years. I was finally out.

DISCHARGED

*Proverbs 23:7 For as he thinks within himself, so
is he. (TPT)*

Through my life, I have learned we all have narratives swirling within us regarding our worth and value. There are those thoughts we are aware of, but other thoughts influence us without our conscious knowledge.

During the ride home with my parents I don't remember a lot of conversation. I had been gone for so long. I was almost 16-years-old now. I know now I was afraid. They had moved to a new home in a different part of the Metropolitan area called Edmond.

I was different. I was no longer the little, confused girl I was when I was institutionalized. I had been traumatized by all I had been presented with in the hospitals. I was a new kind of victim – an angry one.

I was traumatized by being away from my family, harmed by not having one person I felt I could trust, crushed by the torment of the questions, confusion, and professional interventions and crippled by the diagnosis' and manifestations of those I was introduced to during this journey.

And I was shocked by my own response to it all - the anger, the running, the self-mutilation, abuse of others, and the violence of being restrained.

I was paralyzed by the constant message and my deeply felt belief there was something very wrong with me which required mental hospitals, courtrooms, judges, psychiatrists, psychologists, counseling, being locked up and kept away from others at all costs.

The mental terror believing I might be "crazy" - there was something very wrong with me which isn't necessarily wrong with everyone else, remained and resonated with me. I still did not trust people and could not accept love at this point.

I was put into the hospitals and institutions very depressed and confused and was released very angry. Where there is no love, there is automatic anger. The confusion and pain continued with each new transition I was forced to make. And now, I was trying to transition back to, so-to-speak, normal life.

I held a false hope with each new move somehow things would get better. But as a man thinketh...

I heard a saying in one of the places I had been, "wherever you go, there you are".

I was finally out of the institutions and moving again. Why wasn't everything magically better? If life is about paying a price, earning my own stripes, hadn't I paid enough?

The reality was, I was no more equipped to face, handle, or deal with life than before I was hospitalized. In fact, life was even more complicated.

Isaiah 53 says: *By His stripes, we are healed.*

Still to me then, a far-off truth.

My stay there in Edmond proved life would just get more and more pain-filled. New home, new school, my brother's addiction and behavior, having been away from my sister so long, on-going friction and misunderstanding with my mom all contributed to this time being unbearable.

And then my dad died.

I didn't have the time, skills, or confidence to adjust to one thing before another traumatic thing would happen. This is our enemy's design to overwhelm us with attack after attack, devastation after devastation until we give up. I recognize it now.

But then, it was crushing defeat after crushing defeat.

My Dad Floyd Dean Saunders; Me at his grave in Edmond, Oklahoma

Not knowing who or doubting who you are leaves you open to spirits of confusion, oppression, and domination, not to mention, predators and perpetrators. Your "door" is opened to all those who desire to manipulate you, use you, decide and tell you who you are to appease their lusts and desires until they are on to their next victim.

An enemy had laid claim to my life, my identity, my freedom, my dignity, my abilities, my personality, my family. I had no boundaries.

I was a sitting duck. My identity at this point was as a victim.

Until you discover and walk in your identity in Christ, you remain a victim to sin, seducers and Satan.

For in Christ all the fullness of the Deity lives in bodily form and in Christ you have been brought to fullness. He is the head over every power and authority. Colossians 2:9-10

My parents put me into public school in Edmond. I was again in a culture shock. I had been going to school in an institution. I was antisocial at this point. I did not know how to handle or conduct myself. I was terrified but didn't understand what was fueling my thoughts and actions. I was extremely vulnerable. I was not able to function in a way which brought success in any area of life.

I walked from class to class but had no interest and was unable to focus. I knew no one when I got there. I was lost even deeper inside myself. A couple people befriended me, one to smoke pot with and the other to fulfill his lust.

If there was hope for my adopted family to stay together, it was shattered when the two men in suits came to the front door.

It was a scene I will never forget. I stood at the marble entrance while Mom received the news. The men informed her dad had passed away from a heart attack due to complications from congestive heart failure.

He had rheumatic fever as a child and it in turn damaged his heart valves. He was 43-years-old. He lived exactly ten years after bi-pass surgery. He was found unresponsive in a hotel room in Woodward, Oklahoma while on a business trip.

My mom turned around and told me.

I immediately walked down the hall to my room and laid on my bed. I was crushed, yet numb.

I operated in such a constant state of survival by this time and continued to have a very hard time allowing myself to feel anything. My reaction as the pain just kept coming was to sink deep inside myself and hide. I was doing my best to deal with losing my dad and life. But I had no skills.

Most learn to deal with things and all do it differently. But I managed to acquire a method to just not deal with things at all but stuff them.

My mom followed me into my room, laid down on my bed beside me, and put her arms around me. I have never forgotten this gesture of comfort she offered at such a desperate time. It was not common for her to show affection of this kind.

She and I had many conversations and confrontations not characterized by this gentleness and thoughtfulness. I am grateful for those few moments.

They sang, "In the Garden" at my dad's funeral. The song has been a comfort ever since when I hear it played or sung.

After dad's funeral Mom devoted most her efforts to completing her college degree in education. She started her degree before my dad died. A lot of time was spent on classes and homework.

With respect to my adoptive family's privacy, I will refrain from any further details about this time.

There were events which took place which were painful for me and for our family.

There was still a lot of ancillary things taking place in my life, abuse of alcohol, drugs, and influence of huffing gas, which were going on around me prior to dad's passing.

I also contribute the sorrow, pain, and grief in which we were all operating under during this time to dad passing away. The effects were far reaching and deeper than can adequately be put into words then or now.

When death occurs either a family turns inward and grieves together or they all go to their own corners and vices, which grow and cause the whole to fall apart.

We fell apart.

During the grief we were all experiencing and the irresponsible, detrimental choices I continued to make, it was explained to me, my dad's death was perceived as being a result of the stress we caused him.

I was shown the door, told to leave, and I would never live there again.

ADDICTION CYCLES

Fools are famous for repeating their errors, like dogs are known to return to their vomit. Proverbs 26:11 (TPT)

The door was shut and locked behind me.

I walked across the street to the neighbor's house and asked to use their phone. Because I had been in an institution for the length of time I had, they assigned me an outpatient therapist upon my release. I knew her. She was the only person I knew to call.

I was on my second one by this time.

My therapist agreed to let me live with her. I braced myself for yet another move and new school. I wore out my welcome here rather quickly.

Moving into a condominium residence in northwest Oklahoma City, my therapist was able to enroll me in Putnam City North High school where I entered my Sophomore year.

Again, I knew no one. But soon I made a few friends.

There were about five to eight of us who spent time together. We hung out at the pizza place down the street from the school and our homes. We drove around listening to Metallica, Nine Inch Nails and Danzig. I was offered marijuana and LSD. I began smoking pot and dropping acid.

One of the guys of our group - sort of the leader - had a band, played bass guitar, and hung out in his garage practicing. He thought it was fun to rob houses and dared me to join in. I followed along on a couple, thinking it would make me look tough and be accepted.

I took on this new 'tough' personae. It made life easier for me. I began having fun, for a little bit. I had a false sense of freedom – doing whatever I wanted, when I wanted.

One of the friends' dad had a liquor closet. We hung out there and I began drinking liquor. I also spotted a bottle of pills in one of the bathrooms one evening after I had nursed a bottle of whiskey enough to be feeling it.

After picking it up, I read the label which said, "for pain".

I said to myself, "I'm in pain – emotional pain - so this is for me". I took what I believe was my first pain pill, perhaps a Lortab because of the blue-colored specks in it. I felt so good on these pills and alcohol. I remember thinking, "If only I could always feel this way!" It was best feeling I had ever experienced.

I was all about feeling high, free, tough and accepted during this time.

I thought I was all those things. I began getting a reputation of being tough, strong, and crazy. I wore leather jackets, tall leather boots, and flannel shirts. I liked it. I owned it.

I was soon introduced to a guy who they described as being 'crazy' too. All our friends agreed he was someone I should meet. We did meet. Crazy and addicted he was.

We hit it off and began spending a lot of time together.

He was 21 years old. I was 16.

More and more I hung out with him and friends. Mostly we smoked pot, drank alcohol, and skipped school. I hung in my sophomore year as long as I could. But with this type of schedule, I just wasn't interested. I couldn't focus or concentrate. I fell so far behind there was no catching up.

The administrators made attempts to ask questions, bring me in the office to talk and put me in other classes. But there was no helping me really.

One afternoon I drove my therapists Z28 without her permission and went to my boyfriend's house. I didn't go back to her condo. I stayed there with him.

She came and got her car later. When I finally came back, she had placed all my belongings out on the porch and I found the door locked. I don't believe I ever saw her or heard from her again.

I moved in with my boyfriend and his mother.

She was an alcoholic and was living a homosexual lifestyle. I had not been introduced to this before. It was shocking to me when it was revealed while I was there, his mother's boyfriend wasn't really her boyfriend, but her girlfriend.

This produced much anger and hostility in my boyfriend, her son. Not long after moving there I called my mom, explaining what was going on to see if I could come home.

The answer was no. She now tells me, she offered to take me to a treatment facility, but I was not ready to go. It was something she had learned, she called "Tough Love".

His mom went out to clubs and came home in the early morning hours, sometimes bringing the "party" home with her after the bars and clubs closed.

There was a place called the "Habana Inn Resort and Club". Apparently, this place was mainly established for and frequented by the homosexual community. People from different walks of life often came home with her. We never knew what would happen with all the intoxication. Sometimes men who dressed like women came home with her, waking us up, talking very loudly and acting boisterous, wearing skirts, high heels, pantyhose, and heavy make-up.

My life at the house, always seemed surrounded by yelling, fighting, drama, and even police. I can still remember her voice yelling my name then, "Barbie! Barbie!, come here Barbie!" Only, it sounded like "Bobby" with her distinct German accent. She came to America from Germany when she was a teenager.

My boyfriend and I continued to drink alcohol, smoke pot, and drop acid while living there. There was so much conflict, depression, deceit, and addiction. I was brought to the house by the police one night after my boyfriend decided he would try and outrun the police, when they flashed their lights at him to pull over.

When they finally cornered us at the end of a road in Rock Knoll housing addition with numerous police cars and helicopters and bright spot lighting on us, they pulled him out first and found a machete between the seats.

They came to my side and pulled me out by my hair through the driver's side window. Always by the hair.

They were yelling and calling us names. They handcuffed me abusively and aggressively, turned me around, then one of them kicked me from behind so hard I fell face first on the street pavement.

Then another placed the sole of his boot at the base of the back of my neck holding my head down, grinding it into the gravel and rocks causing me to inhale dust and debris from the road. After some time, they took me back to my boyfriend's mom's house in the back of the police car. I was a minor.

While living here I got pregnant.

In this dysfunction and chaos, what little personal relationship remained between me and my boyfriend, dwindled to nothing when I decided to have an abortion.

I thought this to be the best decision at this time. I reasoned, "I was adopted and look what I was going through. I didn't want to put a child up for adoption and have them go through what I was. After all, it is legal. And, it's better than bringing a child into this situation".

I didn't know the truth.

The truth God knew us in our mother's womb, He has all the hairs on our head numbered, and He has a plan for us, from the foundation of the world. It was not even something I had heard at this point. I just made the best decisions I could at the time to survive. I truly believed I was protecting my child from my sad, worthless life.

My boyfriend's mom always had a wide variety of medications around. They were pills she took for depression, anxiety, panic attacks, etc.

After the abortion, I reached a point when I couldn't take any more of the addiction, torment, stress and hopelessness. Once again, I swallowed a few handfuls of these type of pills. I laid myself down on the bathroom floor.

The bathroom was brown carpeted. As I took in the foul smell of the bathroom carpet, I was done. I was just ready and waiting to not have to wake up.

Next thing I knew I woke up in a hospital room with tubes in me. There were a couple friends in the room.

I was angry I was still alive - furious because I didn't want this life anymore.

I was still alive to face the pain, the confusion, the shackles which were my constant reminders, I was unlovable. I felt I had nowhere to go, no way out of addiction, no path out of this desperate situation. I went back to live with my boyfriend and his mother in the same house.

After approximately 18 months living with them, my boyfriend went to jail for burglary. After he returned, I watched him stab himself in the abdomen, which he used as a manipulative tactic to prevent me from leaving him.

I saw this as my way out of a desperate and scary situation.

I checked myself in a drug rehabilitation program in downtown Oklahoma City called Drug Recovery Inc. (Ivanhoe). It was considered an adult facility and I was still a minor. They agreed to let me come, but to no avail. I stayed about four months, leaving before I finished the program.

While there, one of the "old-timers" in recovery stood before about a hundred residents all sitting in a circle for a mandatory meeting and said, "Statistics are, only one out of a hundred addicts make it. It means out of this entire room only one of you will make it."

When I heard it, I thought to myself, "I want to be the one!"

Some ideas stuck with me while there. Their program incorporated the 12 steps of AA and NA.

I was introduced to the idea through steps two and three, there may be a God. Except I just could not grasp it. If there was a God, why must I come up with my own understanding of Him?

It just didn't make sense to me. If there was a God who could save us from all this, or set us free, why didn't He just do it? Consequently, I couldn't get past step three.

I'm convinced, as I look back on attempts like these to get clean and sober, we may want a lot of things for our life. Yet, without a relationship with Jesus and the power of the Holy Spirit, we might desire a lot of things but ultimately, still have no power within ourselves to accomplish them.

> *John 14:6 Jesus explained, "I am the Way, I am the Truth, and I am the Life. No man comes next to the Father except through union with me. To know me is to know my Father too.*

I really wanted to be clean and sober. I did not want my life the way it was. I did not like the way things were going. I just kept running into a brick wall. Getting up and falling down, getting up and falling from one level and depth of darkness to another.

Leaving the drug rehab meant I was homeless - again.

ANOTHER DEPTH OF DECEPTION, DARKNESS, DETOX

Whoever walks in the dark does not know where
they are going. John 12:35 (NIV)

He was an old 'connection' who sold cocaine.

I called. He agreed to let me move in with him and his mother. She ran a psychic line in her home I later discovered was a cover for what was once considered an escort service, which is just a fancy way of saying prostitution.

Years later I learned what I would soon walk into unknowingly is considered a form of sex slavery and trafficking.

From the time I woke up until the time I passed out, I was high or intoxicated.

I did drugs to relieve the pain of my circumstances and choices and all it did was create more and more pain and dangerous circumstances. I could see part of the cycle. I just didn't have the power to get out.

It wasn't long before his mom said it was time for me to go, but not without giving me a "job opportunity". She told me to go meet with two men in the same apartment complex who had a job for me. Since I had no other options or jobs available to help support me, I agreed. I was 17-years-old.

Sophomore, Putnum City North, Oklahoma City – High School Class Picture. I was soon living in sexual slavery with the two older men.

I'll never forget the lingering image of the fear on her son, now my boyfriend's face, pleading with me. "You don't know what you are getting yourself into," he said.

He didn't provide me with any more information about it.

He walked after me and at one point, grabbed my arm and begged me not to go up there. He didn't explain his protest, only made several sincere attempts to change my mind.

If I had only known what he was alluding to, trying desperately to convince me and warn me about. I pulled away and resisted. I needed to survive. I put on my tough front.

I told myself on the way to the apartment I had to do this. If I didn't, I was going to be homeless again. I didn't have anywhere to go. I desperately needed a job. I was actually, somewhat excited about finding legitimate employment instead of spending my time drinking and drugging.

I walked up the stairs and knocked on the apartment door number I had been given. I was taken aback by the very large, obese older man who answered and invited me in the apartment. Reluctantly, I walked in.

I still had no knowledge to this date of two existing kingdoms-one characterized by light and another thrives in darkness.

I found out soon enough one was 56-years-old and the other 43-years-old. Being 17, it was as if I stepped into the very presence of evil.

Another and new depth of darkness – a level of despair I had just stepped into. There was a distinct atmosphere of what I know now to be deception, perversion, and lust.

The older of the two took charge and directed me to a table in the kitchen to sit down. He sat down while the other man, who had answered the door, sat in the living room area. He continued to stare at me. The older man set a deck of cards in front of me on the table saying, "shuffle. Show us your shuffling skills".

I picked up the cards and shuffled the several ways my parents had taught me when our family would play cards at the lake cabin when I was younger.

He said I'd be dealing cards for the American Legion. He then said, "Go get ready, we'll pick you up later and discuss the rest of the job description over dinner".

I went back to the other apartment where I'd been staying. I showered, got ready to go out for dinner. My boyfriend tried a few more protests about me going for this deal. But, once again, he didn't explain why. I simply saw this card dealing as an opportunity to take care of myself.

The two men picked me up in the evening in a new burgundy rag top Lincoln. I got in the back seat and sat down, feeling and smelling the leather. As they drove off, the questions began.

"Do you have a father," one of them asked me. "Where were you raised," the other probed.

Naively I gave them an overview of what I had been through and my situation at the time. Only moments into the drive they knew by my own admission, I had no father, was told to leave where I was living and had nowhere to go.

My history had produced vulnerabilities which set the perfect stage. In hindsight I realize the questions they asked were designed to determine my situation and if there was going to be someone looking for me or coming after me.

They took me to a restaurant where we all ate a steak dinner. After dinner they drove up to a nice hotel. The 56-year-old man, the older of the two, got out and opened the door on my side.

He was a huge man with lots of dark and some white hair. His eyebrows were thick, black and it looked as though he put something on these to stiffen them and shape them like curved horns.

Even though I was operating in the 'tough front', this man was very large and scary. I stepped out of the car. I was somewhat confused. I wondered what we were doing at a hotel.

Eyebrows took my hand and walked me into the hotel through a beautiful and plush registration desk and lobby area. In what seemed like slow motion, we winded through a hall and in and out of an elevator, down another hall into a large, nice room. He sat down on the couch where there were yellow legal pads of paper lying there.

We were alone. I walked around the room. He motioned for me to come over and sit down by him on the couch.

I did. He began showing me his paperwork full of numbers. He briefly attempted to explain what all the numbers meant and how he worked his business. He had lots of "betters" who bet money on football games. There were large amounts of money listed on those pages. It was page after page of names and numbers.

After some time, I got up from the couch and walked to the other side of the room and turned around. His demeanor changed. He got very stern, very straight forward.

He told me to strip. I was terrified and went into survival mode. I knew it well. I did what he told me to do.

People have asked me, but more importantly, I have asked myself, "Why didn't you run? Why didn't you walk out? Why didn't you pick up the phone and call someone?"

Today, I understand this phenomenon. Without a foundation, and even if I had possessed the sense of self value or self-respect, there was no one to call and there was nowhere to go.

I was set up. As sure as a horse herded through a winding, narrowing canyon, I was trapped.

There I was "turning my first trick", as some would call it, at 17 with a 56-year-old old man; all for survival, food, clothes, a place to live, and eventually, for drugs.

He and the other man took me to live with them for a short time in a condo in Clinton, Oklahoma. They continued to make money gambling. I continued to drink alcohol and remain intoxicated from the time I woke up to the time I passed out.

This new depth of shame I endured to live in and maintain this environment is not something I try to think about often, much less describe. I wanted to die. The sooner I could accomplish it through the least painful way I could, the better.

This was my prevailing thought. My only hope out of this shame and darkness was to stay messed up. Drinking and drugs altered my state of mind and emotion. I decided I would do this until I die.

I intuitively knew the gambling money paid for the condo, car, and living expenses. The men took me to a beauty shop and boutique in Clinton, Oklahoma City and Las Vegas. They paid the ladies in shops, telling them to do my hair, make-up, manicure, and pedicure. The older man paid for it all. The other man, he drove.

Eyebrows bought me silk jackets, purses, clothes, and shoes. As if this was sufficient recompense for being his teenage girl sex-slave. The "life", it is sometimes called.

He demanded I look sophisticated and sexy when he took us out. I'll never forget the glances we received and stares from on-lookers in public places. It was a look as if to say, "Why is this young of girl with these two older men." Anyone in their right mind would have recognized there was something not quite right with this picture and situation. But no one said or did anything; only stared.

After some time (I lost any concept of time between the emotional trauma and drugs and alcohol), the other man who drove and lived with us had been bringing me pills and drugs.

He expected sexual 'favors and services' in return for my living expenses. When the two of them would leave on trips, he would drive me over to southside Oklahoma City and drop me off at a house and told me to stay there until he got back. It could be two days, two weeks or longer.

I learned later he gave money to the women who lived there. She mainlined and turned heroine. It was called "black tar". She showed me how to either crush pills to cold shake dilute, or heat and draw up heroin in a spoon. She hit the vein in my left arm the first time. After a while, however, she informed me I'd have to learn to hit myself. She wasn't going to do it for me anymore.

The men also flew me out to Las Vegas with them. We stayed at Caesar's Palace. There were a lot of lights and people. They expected me to dress up and they would take me to live shows and dinner. On the main floor of the hotel there were row after row of slot machines. I sat down and played those for some time.

No sooner had I sat down, a waitress approached and asked me what kind of beverage I would like. I ordered a White Russian not really thinking they would actually bring me one. After-all, I was 17-years-old. But they brought me one, and another one, and another one. It was free, unlimited drinks on the house while playing the machines.

The first time I sat down, it didn't take long before an alarm and lights on top of the machine I was playing went off! It frightened me at first but then someone next to me said, "You won!" A person soon came and counted out six one hundred-dollar bills in my hand.

I was already addicted to heroin, cocaine, and craving the needle.

I could drink to take away the edge of withdrawals while in Nevada, but I couldn't wait to get back to the dope house to shoot.

It was really the only thing left which would get me to a state where I didn't have to think or care. Nothing could take away the shame of this life and pain of the past completely. But it numbed it for a while. Now I had won six bills which is all I could think about.

When we returned, we moved to the new, lovely home. We were now in northwest Oklahoma City living in a large, expensive home there in a neighborhood near Putnam City North High School.

It had a pond with fish in the backyard. Sometimes I would stand at the edge of the pond. As I stood there I could see in the not so far distance, at the end of the neighborhood, the high school I had attended. It was not long ago I was struggling to get from class to class. Now, I was enslaved to two men, drugs, and alcohol.

It was like being in Bethany Pavilion just right down the road from the home where I grew up before I was institutionalized for so long. There was such a comparison, as well as, a contrast of standing in a darker place longing for what had been difficult too.

It can always get worse. It would be years before I would learn and experience I could be free, forgiven, and full of God's love, joy, peace, and purpose.

I was still obligated to 'service' the older man. He seemed basically satisfied with the arrangement, until he began to get more and more aggravated with my constant intoxication. He'd tell me I reminded him of his "son the druggy" and I had no class. He became extremely verbally cruel, mean, and degrading. There came a day when he no longer required me to pleasure him.

He then started to bring girls from Dallas there to service him and then pimp them out. One black girl came and talked me into putting the powder cocaine I used for mainlining in a pot on the stove and cooking it somehow with something. She liked to smoke it in a pipe. She called it "rocking it up".

Nothing else ever took me from my reality so quickly and thoroughly as using IV drugs. I thought at the time this method was a waste of perfectly good dope. Besides, she was always trying to correct how I was holding the pipe, how to and how not to light it up, turn the pipe, and suck on the pipe. Whateva. Just give me a spoon and syringe.

Since the older man was 'done' with me, the younger man assumed possession of me. I went from staying on one side of the house to the other. This seemed to cause much conflict and arguments between the men

It was 1992. The year I should have graduated high school.

I began stealing hundred-dollar bills from the men after they fell asleep. Being used and using others characterizes this lifestyle. I took the extra vehicle from north side of the city to south side to the dope house, so I could get high. I stayed high.

I shared needles with anyone and everyone who came in and out of the dope house. I didn't care. I was drugged up, raped, and ripped off in this environment.

By this point I frequently thought about wanting to die. This was always the answer to me. The sooner the better and in the least painful way, was how I saw it. It was the only way out of a worthless, hopeless, miserable life.

DETOX

Before I accomplished killing myself, I got very sick. I was sick to the point I could barely stand up or walk. I was mentally, physically, and emotionally sick.

I was spiritually lost in a world of sin and degradation.

The younger man dropped me off at Griffin Memorial hospital in Norman. Here they diagnosed me with two forms of liver disease. The physician explained with a serious yet compassionate face it was already in a chronic state in my liver. I already had approximately a 70-year-old liver. He went on to convey if I did not quit doing drugs and drinking I would be dead by the time I was 30. I was 18-years-old.

As I looked into the eyes of the doctor while he spoke those words, I experienced a flood of relief. Even though 30 still seemed like a long way off from 18, I was relieved to hear I was much closer to my goal. I stayed at the hospital quite some time as they treated me.

The detoxification process was brutal. I sweated. I slept for days. I could not eat for some time. I was nauseous in the awake moments and vomited. It was painful to walk or even sit.

My upper right abdominal area hurt to touch. My stools were gray. I stayed in a bed for days. I was extremely weak, and it was if every cell, muscle, organ, bone in my body hurt and ached.

Physiological withdrawal was miserable. However, the medication and support they provided helped me through it. I, gradually, was able to join others in an open area. I met a young man there who confided he was there due to a diagnosis of HIV. I begged him to share a needle with me. I figured death would be sure and sooner. He refused.

Upon my discharge, I called my mom telling her of the diagnosis and treatment asking her if I could come home.

The answer remained the same. No.

I had nowhere to go.

MARRIAGE AND CHILDREN

I contacted the younger of the two men who had brought me to the hospital. He agreed to come get me and take me over two hours away from the city, where he was from, to Mooreland, Oklahoma.

He and the other man parted ways after the gambling money ran out. There were a few occasions when he had asked me to marry him. I thought he was joking. He was twenty-four years older than me. I wasn't in any shape and our situations were hardly the kind of groundwork to enter marriage. I blew off his proposals.

Living together I soon got pregnant. I had made the wrong decisions up to this point. Having this baby seemed a good place to start. Again, he asked me to marry him. I saw no other options for survival with a baby on the way. We married while I was pregnant with my first daughter. I was 19–years-old.

In January of 1995, I delivered Renee' my first daughter. Twenty-two months later in October of 1996, I delivered Deanna, my second daughter.

As you can imagine, the both of us coming from these two lifestyles created many issues.

Yet, I remained sober and clean from all alcohol and drugs during my pregnancies.

I delivered beautiful baby girls. I love them with all my heart. I was also scared and overwhelmed by the responsibility.

My first daughter had what they called "colic". She cried almost non-stop for days. I was in hard labor for a long time with her. It was very difficult.

My mom came and stayed with me the first week after my first two girls were born, allowing me some time to rest and recover. She cooked and cleaned while there, but our relationship was still perfunctory. She did come and do this for me and I appreciated it.

Giving birth to my second daughter was a lot less painful and long. She seemed calmer and slept more often. Again, Mom came and stayed to help the first week after she was born.

One day a lady named Linda came by where we lived and invited me to her church and prayed for me. I was sitting on the edge of my loveseat and she was sitting on the edge of my couch. It was a tiny ray of light.

So, I went to the First Baptist Church in Mooreland a few times.

One of those times I walked down front, wanting what Pastor Jim so passionately spoke about. He prayed with me. I remember being blown away thinking, "Is this really real? Is everything this man is saying real? Is there really a God? Is there really a God who loves me?"

The verse of scripture I hid in my heart was from one of his sermons:

"Well-done good and faithful servant"
(Matthew 25:21).

This phrase touched my heart. I longed to hear well-done from my Father. Every time the Word of God intersected my life it was a powerful force.

I was even baptized while pregnant with my second daughter. But I didn't understand who Jesus was, why I needed Him, or how He could change my life.

There was still no real change going on within me.

While expecting our first baby, we were told we were having a boy. When we had a girl, their dad seemed disappointed. He didn't help with her or have much to do with her. He stayed gone most the time saying he was working. I was overwhelmed.

From the beginning, except his mother and aunt, the rest of his family were unkind and acted very rude toward me and my daughters. I didn't understand this. It hurt me deeply. I learned there was some talk from his side of the family, my girls may not belong to him, but perhaps to a different man.

The rejection I had struggled with most my life, I continued to face here and now, and was watching it happen to my daughters. I loved my girls so very much, yet I began to identify with rejection which continued and remained.

In addition, I found it stressful taking care of two little ones while he was mostly gone. When he happened to come home he was unavailable. After we married, he would call me names, spit on me, ridicule, and degrade me verbally. He called me a slut and a whore.

I remember the looks when we would be together in public.

Being married and having children with a man much older than I had its dynamics. Among them were comments, at times innocently inquiring if he was my father and/or assuming he was my children's grandfather. I didn't know how to deal with it all or with anything.

The best way I knew how to deal with rejection, stress, pain, disappointment, fear, abuse, triggers, life, was to run, drink, or do drugs to try and relieve it temporarily

ARRESTS AND INTERROGATIONS

Their father finally came home from what he said was business. Feeling locked up, I needed to get out of the house and away for a while. I took the vehicle to Woodward sometimes. I often went to bars there or to someone's house to get drunk or smoke pot. Once the drinking started, I lost track of time. On a few occasions I stayed out all night drinking.

I would come home the next day still drunk. He would take the girls to his mother during these binges.

One episode, I had been up all-night drinking and took some pain pills. I fell asleep on the highway on my way home. When I fell asleep, the vehicle I was driving veered right. When I awoke, there was blood all over me. I was slouched to the right. My nose had cracked after hitting the steering wheel. I managed to get out the driver's side and waved at a car. They pulled over, let me in the back seat of their car, and took me around the corner to where I lived. The girl's father took me to a doctor for pain pills and said he could re-break and re-set my nose at a later date.

I was later charged with my first felony "Leaving the scene of an accident to avoid detection". I had to appear in court and was sentenced to fines, costs and counseling. I attended outpatient counseling sessions, private counseling and some group sessions in Woodward, Oklahoma.

Times of sobriety got shorter and shorter. I began using the drug of choice in the next closest town at the time, Methamphetamine, commonly known as crank. I did not drink or do drugs around my daughters, so I would leave them mostly with their grandma or dad during these times.

I was lost, unsettled, frustrated, and scared. I continued to try and find relief and escape through alcohol, drugs, and running.

During this time, I took a trip to Oklahoma City. I had not done heroin since the brutal detoxification at Griffin Memorial Hospital. I was drinking beer all the way there. I scored some heroin from an old contact, boiled it in a spoon, dropped the cotton in, drew it up and slammed it. I was told I fell unconscious before I could take the needle out of my arm.

I awoke in a house sometime later. I recall being told it had been a couple days. I suffered what was thought to be lack of oxygen. I couldn't put sentences together. It took weeks for me to get my cognitive ability back. It was the last time I ever did heroin.

Also, during this time, I was questioned on a few occasions by law enforcement in Woodward county. Once by a private detective for the District Attorney's office named Butch. I was asked why I was with this man? How did I meet him? Did I know he was a drug dealer? Did I know he was an accused pedophile? What could I tell them about him? The confrontation had less to do with me upon questioning, as it would end up turning to interrogation about my husband.

This line of questioning increased my fear of him.

I had always held a fear of him because of the circumstances under which we met and lived. It stirred up memories of how we met. Pictures I had found of him and young girls in his apartment. Stories he had told me, he had been a part of a murder during his ten years living in Las Vegas. He also had intimated he had been present during another shooting of a man from the back in the middle of a field over a drug deal. He told me of being 'busted' with 250,000 Quaaludes in a private plane and kilos of cocaine by the Feds but had not ever been arrested due to what he called an illegal search and seizure and him turning state's evidence on some of his partners.

He would say these things reinforcing his belief he could do anything he wanted, his way, and get by with it. He did admit one time to getting 7-years' probation after getting busted again by selling a ½ pound of powdered sugar (thought to be crank) to an undercover agent (Most of this information can be found in a written testimony pamphlet written by himself he eventually shared in public settings).

He also described a trial he went through after being on the Kansas turnpike in 1989. He said one night he was pulling a hay wagon when the truck blew a radiator hose. When the wrecker he had called for was pulling him back to the station, he couldn't handle the hay wagon and truck together. He had a pipe wrench and tried to loosen the hay wagon off the hitch. A Camaro went under the hay wagon and cleared it. Then, a van of six people hit the back of the hay wagon and the three people in the front seat were killed.

My fear of him grew.

I never really knew the whole truth. I had my doubts about everything he told me and what others would tell me about him, including law enforcement who I didn't trust either.

However, during the moments when I was most honest with myself, the compilation of stories and my own experience with this man all pointed to me and my children being in a dangerous position.

Anytime his name was mentioned around the area, it would bring fearful looks and angry comments about who he was, things he had done, what he was capable of. It all instilled a deeper fear in me. I began to wake up to the possibility of being a victim of sorts.

I didn't like the idea of being a victim. I desperately tried to create a mental scenario more acceptable to me, on some level dismissing the truth in order to function. I later learned some victims don't self-identify as victims. I would literally go in and out of facing reality. This is what the drugs assisted in accomplishing. But not for long.

It's as if the frail human mind does not readily accept things like this, especially about people closest to them, namely family members. Many times, the mind seeks denial over painful truths. For me, there seemed to be no way out.

This realization sparked unspeakable fear in me. It also stirred up the all too familiar survival and anger; anger which motivated me to want out! It was an anger which wanted me to do anything I needed to do to get my children out and to fight for them.

For the first time, my anger was motivating me instead of harming me.

I knew I wouldn't be able to leave for good without help.

I remember him talking about a man on a few occasions. It was a man who worked for him at one time - the only man he said he was ever really afraid of and would never want to mess with. I called the man.

We began meeting in Woodward. I soon moved in with him. My goal was to get away from their dad with my girls.

I was survival focused.

Single focused, I drove by my girls' grandmothers house and, to my relief, both my daughters were outside in the yard. I stopped and got them into the car and drove off. I did not bother to deal with or speak to anyone before taking them as it usually resulted in an argument, and them trying to hold and keep my daughters away from me.

In my mind I was getting my girls and I away from a bad situation to move on. They stayed the night with me at this man's home for only a short time. I could tell they were scared and uneasy to be there.

Despite desperately desiring to, I had no permanent arrangements made to back up the decision to take care of them and have my girls live with me. They ended up back with their father and his family.

I was tormented and frustrated I was in no position to safely and fully support my girls and myself. The routine of rough road continued. Defeat and despair remained.

Then the man I was living with mentioned he could get me some meth and did so. While living there I was mainlining meth. He also began drinking and relapsed smoking crack. He began behaving angrily and the situation scared me as well.

Going to this man for help was another failed attempt at getting free. I lost a lot of weight using and going from place to place scoring dope. I began meeting dealers and others using crank.

I was at a hotel room in Woodward one night called the Red-Carpet Inn, now known as Red Country Inn, where there had been a huge pile of meth. The dealer was at the table cutting it and bagging to sell. He also had a gun on the table.

I had an unusual sense of the presence of evil once again which remains etched in my mind.

There were a handful of others in the hotel room. Someone opened the front door of the hotel room and a police car pulled up and they gave the officer some of the dope, came back in, and shut the door. I realized then the police were involved in the doing and dealing in Woodward.

Fear continued to grip my heart. It was 1998.

One girl in the hotel room was so high she was walking around the room without any clothes. The men in the room were going in and out of the bathroom with her for extended periods of time.

I wanted to leave.

I started to get up slowly and move to the end of the bed where I was sitting. At the same time one of the other women in the room came and sat beside me and whispered, "Are you (she said his first and last name) wife?"

I moved my head up and down very slowly, affirmatively.

She continued to whisper, "I am wearing a wire right now. Did you know he is trying to have you killed?" Tremendous fear went through me. I remembered he had tried at it before, revealed by the confession of the man he had paid money to do it. There are no words to describe how scared I became right then in the room.

I slowly began to stand up, wanting to make my way to the door yet terrified someone in the room might shoot me or rape me.

When I did so the large man from the opposite corner, who appeared extremely intoxicated and had just come from the bathroom, began yelling at me. With a slight hesitation, I went ahead and opened the door and walked out.

I was almost paralyzed from fear.

A young man followed me out. I continued to walk around the corner toward the parking lot. Before we left the hotel parking lot, police cars, one after another, began turning in.

A certain kind of terror I will never forget continued to overtake me.

Six to eight law enforcement cars of different kinds headed our way and began circling me. The guy who followed me out ran. I just stood there as they all circled me with their vehicles.

They came to a stop.

One by one officers began getting out of the cars holding large black flashlights, clubs, and other things in their hands. First thing they asked, "Where is he?" (they said his first and last name). I told them I didn't know. I explained I had left and had not seen him in some time.

Something was said about taking me in for questioning and witness protection. I told one of them, "All I want is my babies". They put me in one of the enforcement vehicles and took me to the city office. The private investigator for the District Attorney's office continued asking me questions. They always had a lot of questions about him. Then let me go.

After this lengthy interrogation, I walked out of the city offices. First thing I saw was a church across the street. I walked across and sat down on a pew bench in front of this church, under a light.

I began trying to process all which had just happened. I began contemplating about God and wondering if He was legitimately real, and if I'd ever be free to live a normal life without fear. A life without the need to run or hide or escape.

I decided I would need to try and get away from the man I was living with and the new detrimental situation I sought out as an attempt to get out of the situation with the girls' father. I took another man over to the residence where I was staying to try and retrieve personal clothing items. I came in the back-sliding door, which was my habit.

When I came in the trailer, he began attacking me, punching me over and over. The other man came through another back door with a shovel. He was a lot shorter than this man and when the other man saw the shovel he reached for it and threw it aside. The smaller, shorter man then grabbed his private parts. I learned later the man had to be taken to the hospital to have the area stitched. We then left the trailer with the man holding himself, bleeding, and without my belongings.

Not long after this I began getting arrested. I was arrested on multiple felony counts including Possession of Cocaine and Burglary First Degree and subsequent misdemeanor charges involved in the mix of and under these primary counts.

I would get out on bond for one arrest and charges, only to get arrested again for something else. Truth is, I don't remember all the details to some of the events prior to the arrests because I was deep in addiction, running in fear, and survival.

I was lost in darkness.

After witnessing the police involved in the drugs and dealing, when I would get arrested I would announce in a loud voice in the jail the cops were crooked and vocalize my mistrust, "What's really going on around here?"

I was told by one of the Sheriffs, when I would calm down from a heightened episode of anxiety attacks and fear, they brought me in one of the times to keep me safe. Word on the street was I was going to be killed and "gotten rid of".

Some of the charges were eventually dismissed with fines and costs. However, the DA prosecuted me on Cocaine and Burglary charges. These are both considered First Degree felonies.

With the first few arrests and charges, I would use the pay phone in the jail cell to call my girls father, who I was still married to. He would come post bond. I would walk out of the jail, get into his truck only for him to hand me a bag of dope. Within hours of my release I would be high again. I took it, but it scared me he was the one offering it.

One of these times he took me with him and drove for hours and hours to one of his job sites where one of his crews were building a Sonic. On the way he pulled into a gas station in a remote area just passing through. He handed me dope and a syringe, but we didn't have any water or liquid to break it down and shoot it up.

I went into the public restroom which only had a toilet, no sink or running water.

Filth layered the gas station bathroom. The smell of stale urine bored into my senses, as I dipped the point of the syringe into the toilet water to fill it.

On my knees in front of the toilet bowl, I pushed a stream of water from the syringe into the spoon I had placed on the concrete floor. The meth dissolved into the liquid. Using the end of my syringe, I crushed the remaining crystal-like rocks. I ripped off a small piece of filter from a cigarette, rolled it up in a ball between my fingers then dropped it down into the thickening solution.

As I watched the cotton absorb and expand, I lowered the point of the needle on top, drew up the dope, then lifted it in vertical view. I thumped the clear cylinder as a few remaining bubbles rushed to the top. I placed the loaded syringe between my teeth and bit the barrel while I used my shirt as a tourniquet twisting it tight around my arm causing my antecubital vein to swell to the surface of my skin.

During the process of this repetitive ritual and just before I injected the evil into my blood stream, I thought to myself, "This is what I do. This is who I am."

Kneeling on the floor, doing the dope with everything already going on in my life, represented a bottom for me. Literally stone-cold bottom floor. I kept finding myself on the bottom. The bottom of the courthouse in a jail cell, and now hitting bottom on a dirty bathroom floor at a gas station.

I was disgusted with myself. I didn't care because I was also in such a fog. I only wanted out and my out was to use any means necessary to get high and try and remove myself from the present reality and trap I was in. Emotionally, I felt like a stone, nothing. It wouldn't be long before I'd be arrested on something else. I accumulated "stacked" charges as a result. Open cases wouldn't get closed and sentenced before I would receive more charges.

After being picked up by the police and arrested, the officer would take me in and turn me over to the jailers. Conyetta, Jennifer, and later Saunie were the female jailers.

They were kind to me despite the destructive cycle I was repeating.

One would ask about thirty minutes of questions, put their findings in a computer, while another would check in anything on my person left from the run and binge. Then to the bathroom where one of the female officers would strip search and frisk me checking for contraband. They always took my bra.

Then came the oranges. To this day, I do not wear orange. It's an understood thing in my family and a kind of running joke. Funny, not funny. No orange, if it can be prevented, in the house. Orange represents the old life.

After changing into the infamous orange county jail uniform and orange plastic flip flops which would be my attire for the duration of my stay, it was time for fingerprints.

Stepping up to have my fingerprints taken each time I was arrested became like stepping up on the scales at the doctor's office. About the same sinking feeling, as well. Then the mugshot to match. I learned to try and prolong this process as long as possible. After the logistics came the inevitability of being locked up in the first cell.

Over and over the dark, musty 8.5 x 12-foot cement room became my temporary home. Being locked up in jail is like running full speed right into a brick wall.

I hated it.

It was all too familiar cycle I had stepped into at age thirteen. Run and keep running until something bigger and stronger stops you.

The long arm of the law was big enough and strong enough to slow me down and stop me for a while. However, not strong enough to break the force driving me to perpetually make the decisions I was making.

Not strong enough to break the chains of addiction. Not strong enough to cancel the generational curse passed down to me.

Not strong enough to override the curse of witchcraft and rebellion spoken over me. Not strong enough to heal from the wounds and pain of abuse and abandonment from family.

Not strong enough to restore my fragile, fragmented mind. Not strong enough to deliver me from darkness, depression, and despair.

I was too hopeless and helpless to get out of this mess of reality.

Therefore, no one will be declared righteous in his sight by observing the law; rather, through the law we come conscious of sin. (Romans 3:19)

What shall we say then? Is the law sin? Certainly not! Indeed, I would not have known what sin was except through the law. For I would not have known what coveting really was if the law had not said, "Do not covet." (Romans 7:7)

In approximately one year I racked up multiple felony charges and was sitting in a jail cell awaiting trial. My husband had filed for divorce and I lost temporary custody of my two girls.

The last time I had appeared before the judge he looked directly at me and strictly stated, "Young lady if you were to be convicted on all these counts, you are looking at about sixty years in the state penitentiary".

In the jail cell I was experiencing vivid feelings of total despair with suicidal thoughts consuming me. I had lost everything which meant anything to me.

I had struggled with suicidal suggestions since I was thirteen years old. The confusion and frustration reached another peak, while incarcerated facing more and longer imprisonment.

I felt trapped.

Only now, my babies would have to grow up without a mom. I couldn't stand the thought.

I was addicted and couldn't stop. I didn't know what to do or how to make things right. Confusion and despair was so pressing and tormenting I would literally beat my head against the steel cell door over and over again until my forehead would bleed, then later bruise.

I didn't want to be in this situation and didn't know how my life got here.

They offered wool blankets for covers in jail. Turns out I'm seriously allergic to wool. I acquired a horrible skin infection during one of my long stays. I didn't know what was happening right away. But after some miserable bit of time, red, itchy, painful areas and sores with puss appeared all over my body and didn't go away.

Finally, an officer at the jail took me to Woodward hospital in cuffs. I was placed in a room type space and told to sit on the bed behind a drawn curtain. The officer went away for a little while. I was the only one behind my area of curtain.

While waiting, a Native American looking woman with scrubs on came around the curtain. I assumed she was a nurse. She appeared like a nurse. With the kindest, loving look she gently touched my arm and said, "Don't worry, everything is going to be ok". It was extremely comforting.

I was living in so much fear, torment, anxiety, hopelessness, and despair at the time. The officer came back soon after this. A doctor and another nurse came in as well. Before I left I asked if I could speak to the Native American nurse. I planned to thank her for her kindness, encouragement, and thoughtfulness. Her presence and touch calmed and genuinely reassured me. The medical folks just looked at one another, then at me and said emphatically, "There is no Native American Nurse who works here."

I didn't quite know what to make of this incident then. Now I understand I experienced an angelic encounter in the form of a nurse bringing me some hope.

I was taken back to jail with some medication to resolve the infection. One day, a jailer pushed a bag of items to me through the bean hole. I reached in the sack and pulled out a tube of toothpaste and deodorant. Those were valued commodities in jail.

There was also a picture of my two daughters. I began to cry. I missed them so much and was crushed they were without their mom.

In 1998, the cells at the Woodward county jail were ironically located in the basement of the courthouse, silently yet intently confirming what most of the women believed about ourselves. We were the bottom of society. Only deserving of the basement where all the endless daily dust would settle.

Oh, the shame of it all! With each new arrest I was one step closer to complete brokenness.

One night I was laying on the lower bunk. I usually was given the top bunk because of my height but this time around I was on the bottom. My cry on the thin mattress was no shallow thing. It arose from the depths of my being, from my soul, causing me to literally shake from the misery. As high as it reached was the indication of the depths from which it came.

I believe God heard my cry. The genuine repentance God in His mercy grants to one who is truly broken was beginning to be extended to me. Just as God heard the desperate cries birthed out of bitter bondage from human slaves in Egypt I read about later, my cries reached Father's ears.

He continued drawing me to Himself and making a way for my escape and deliverance.

Exodus 2:23-25 NIV

> *During that long period, the king of Egypt died.*
> *The Israelites groaned in their slavery and cried out,*
> *and their cry for help because of their slavery went*
> *up to God. God heard their groaning and he*
> *remembered his covenant with Abraham, with Isaac*
> *and with Jacob. So, God looked down on the*
> *Israelites and was concerned about them.*

I tried my best to make sure no one else in the cell could hear me cry. But I assure you, God heard. And, He responded!

Psalm 40:1-2 NIV

> *I waited patiently for the LORD; he turned to*
> *me and heard my cry. He lifted me out of the slimy*
> *pit, out of the mud and mire; he set my feet on a rock*
> *and gave me a firm place to stand.*

Oh, the consequences! When I first began to be arrested I saw it only as a speed bump on the road of the lifestyle I was trapped in.

But time would prove it was needed to not only protect me but pry my eyes open and jolt my conscious, causing me to see what I was doing and what truly was happening. Who I was affecting and where I was headed.

The arrests, charges, and incarcerations were a tool in the hands of a Holy, merciful, and patient God who soon brought me to repentance, dealt with, and overcame the destructive force slowly but surely destroying my life.

I would soon learn this force is called sin. Romans 3:23 states:

> *For all have sinned and fallen short of the glory*
> *of God.*

81

Finally, my actual legitimate diagnosis revealed of every person who ever lived, who is alive now, and will ever live. The bible calls it sin.

There is only one cure. One answer. One force. One power stronger than sin.

The blood of Jesus. JESUS!!

This is where I began reading a little Bible which had been placed in my cell. I began reading in Psalms. He, who I now know to be David, who wrote the Psalms, talked a lot about enemies. I related with the Word of God right away. It seemed I had acquired quite a few enemies, namely myself.

Due to the multiple arrests I had become familiar with the routine. One day I was taken in handcuffs to the courtroom for one of several types of court appointments. Consisting of either arraignment, preliminary hearing, trial, or sentencing.

I was led up to the loft where the prisoners sat during court. Danny took one of his keys and removed the handcuffs. One day the shackles. I sat with my head down waiting for the judge to enter and take the bench.

This day I dared to lift my head to look out a window at the southwest corner of the courtroom as the bailiff pronounced, "All Rise" while the Judge made his way to the bench.

I was trying to catch view of some light. When I did I saw Pastor Jim. The Pastor who preached the sermon from a passage in the bible which spoke to me about a job well done by a good and faithful servant. Who had also prayed with me and baptized me over a year prior.

I could feel tears welling up in my eyes.

When I saw him sitting there, it spoke deeply to me. It was like a ray of bright light in a very dark place.

His presence was like the very presence of God saying to me, "I'm here for you Barbara. I'm reaching out to you. I love you and I want you. I see you. Remember, I'm real. I want to save you. I will rescue you. Barbara, I am calling you by name"

It spoke too many things for me to find words to express.

Pastor Jim simply showed up for my court hearing. However, to me it had inexpressible encouragement and comfort.

It gave me hope. Hope is priceless.

Father God was making His presence known to me in such obvious, powerful, recurring ways during this time, it all seemed to be building up to something. I even had the thought God might be trying to tell me I was going to die soon because of the feelings of utter weariness I was having which seemed to be pointing to the end.

Praise God it was an end but not THE end.

In fact, it proved to be death to my old self and birth to my new life in Christ.

RANSOMED

[ran-suhm]

Noun - the redemption of a prisoner,
slave, or

kidnapped person, of captured
goods, etc., for a

price. the sum or price paid or
demanded;

Dictionary.com

SENTENCING AND SALVATION

For even the Son of Man did not come to be served, but to serve, and to give His life as a RANSOM for many. Mark 10:45

Originally, I signed a plea bargain agreement presented to me from the District Attorney's office as a first offer. DA Bouse's offer was to enter Department of Corrections (DOC). Essentially, I would be serving time in prison. I was to be assigned an inmate number.

To this day I'm not quite clear on what exactly went down in the courtroom as I stood before Judge Marak's bench. I don't remember the specific words which came out of my mouth. I do know I was scared and was even more fearful to go to prison. I had been terrified for quite some time running and addicted, and basically terrorized by the men I was involved with.

I was also angry. Why was I the only one facing prison? How can the men I was around and coming in contact with who were doing and also slinging dope continue to be out on the streets beating the system, or possibly more appropriately stated, working the system?

Mostly, I thought of my girls being without their mom for a very long time.

After the paperwork was signed for me to go to prison it was presented to the court. The Judge looked at me and asked something to the effect 'are you making this decision freely or without being coerced?"

Immediately, I began speaking some things on my mind as if my life depended on it. And in my mind, it did.

I believe the words I said in those moments were referring to surrounding events leading up to my arrests and charges. The police being in on drug deals in the town and how one of the charges was to retrieve my own things from an abusive man's home and being attacked in the process resulting in the burglary charge.

Making sense of the situation was beyond me.

Yes, I had an addiction I was in desperate need of overcoming. But it seemed to me the extent of the charges was a bit trumped up, so they say. One person explained to me it was as if I was being "railroaded".

The first offer was thrown out. I was then led out.

Officer Danny cuffed my hands. We walked out of the courtroom down the hall and as we stepped onto the elevator he glanced down at me, shook his head with a look of disbelief and said, "That was stupid kid".

I responded shocked, "What was stupid?"

He came back, "You basically just insinuated, even accused the District Judge of being involved with, in on, or covering up for illegal activities". I honestly don't remember what I said but I do know I was fighting for my life and my children.

He explained the legal process would now start all over. I had been in jail some months already waiting for my day of sentencing. Now I'd be waiting even longer.

I dismissed the representation the girls' father hired for me. I reasoned he may not have my best interest or the best interest of my children in mind.

Honestly, at this point I trusted no one.

My husband had, after all, offered information to the law which led to at least one of my arrests, if not more.

He filed for divorce knowing I was incarcerated with a stack of charges and there would be no apparent way I could fight for my girls. This would ensure full custody of our children to him. Also, he presented me with drugs when I was in his presence and word on the street was he sold dope, as well. There was also the woman at the hotel room telling me he hired someone to kill me because I was trying to get away from him, as well as, the information the private detectives had given me during questioning sessions. So, there was really no way for me to delude myself any longer regarding the intentions of this man.

I was addicted. I was broken. I was tired, so tired. I was afraid. I was facing time in prison and yet, I continued reading the little Bible in my cell.

There were two ladies who came to visit. They'd kneel in front of the opening in my cell. They called the opening a 'bean hole'. We called them the 'church ladies'. The church ladies came to the jail routinely.

I climbed down from the top bunk and sat on the cement floor in front of the bean hole when they would arrive.

My question for them one day was, "Do you have to go through this hell on earth and then when you die, you can go to heaven and find relief and joy?"

One of them answered, "No, you can ask Jesus to come into your life to be your Savior now. You can know joy and peace right here on earth."

Joy and peace are two things I had not ever known. Not really.

I had believed if I could just die - if I could kill myself somehow - I'd go to heaven and then all the pain, confusion, torment, struggle with addiction, abandonment, homelessness, not knowing who I am, and hurting those I love, would all be over.

I now know if I had died in my sin, having never entered a relationship with Jesus, I would not have gone to heaven. I would have entered to a real place called hell. And it would be eternal, real, hell. Not just the taste of hell I was walking through and sitting in on this earth.

There would be no chance of hope, no more chance at healing.

They moved on down to the next cell. And when they left, it is what I did. Desperate, I leaned against the top bunk, bowed my head and prayed, "God I can't do this anymore. But Jesus if you can, then do it. Come into my life and be my Lord". When I opened my eyes from the prayer, I knew!

My life literally has never been the same ever since!

Through the Word of God, what I know now to be the Spirit of God drawing me, and two ladies of God leading me in the cell, I experienced salvation and was forever transformed.

It has been a process to get where I am today, but this is where it began, my salvation leaning against the steel hardness of the bunk with the miserable, thin mattress.

At my lowest place Jesus found me. He reached me in the pit of my consequences. His love and kindness brought me to genuine repentance and confession which led to my salvation.

> *If you declare with your mouth, "Jesus is Lord,"*
> *and believe in your heart that God raised him from*
> *the dead, you will be saved. For it is with your heart*
> *that you believe and are justified, and it is with your*
> *mouth that you profess your faith and are saved. As*
> *Scripture says, "Anyone who believes in him will*
> *never be put to shame." For there is no difference*
> *between Jew and Gentile—the same Lord is Lord of*
> *all and richly blesses all who call on him, for,*
> *"Everyone who calls on the name of the Lord will be*
> *saved." Romans 10:9-13*

RANSOMED!

Immediately, I began open and free dialogue with God. I poured my heart out expressing what I was thinking and feeling. I was convinced he had sought me out, loved me, and was with me.

I begged Him to not have to go to prison. I intuitively knew if I went to prison, I would not come out the same. I was afraid for myself and for my children.

By the grace of God, the next offer from the District Attorney was considerably less incarceration time. The papers were presented to me by the court appointed attorney at the time, Don Work.

I signed, accepted, and was sentenced to ten years on one felony count and five years on the drug possession charge to run concurrently. It means at the same time.

These offers were considered suspended sentences, which was briefly explained to me and I understood to mean if I was re-arrested for anything I would more than likely do the entire time in prison.

I was also sentenced, and court ordered to a drug and alcohol treatment program. I was required to complete a minimum of a ninety-day program and only had a certain amount of time to do it. It was up to me to find the program and get myself there. I also had a large sum of fines and court costs on a payment schedule.

I realized, as I signed the new plea bargain papers, having been through the judicial process twice now, there must be a God of mercy intervening on my behalf. I also knew there was no way on my own I could stay clean and out of trouble for ten years.

However, I signed what I needed to in the moment to get out of what I was facing. I really thought, as I signed those papers, at some point I would end up doing time in prison. Signing the plea bargain meant I would be credited time served and be able to see my babies.

I was released from jail.

I called and began the arrangements for my youngest daughter and I to go to Waynoka Women and Children's Treatment Center. I wanted and planned to take my oldest daughter, as well.

However, I reluctantly accepted the request by their father's family for her to remain with her grandmother while I focused on treatment and completing this program.

This was a very difficult decision. I always 'fought' for my girls. I knew if I didn't complete this program I could go to prison and my children and I could be separated for who knows how long or, even worse, grow up without me. If I could I would never allow it to happen. I would fight or die trying not to let it happen.

I waded through nagging negative thoughts and subtle suggestions where maybe my children were better off with someone else. I heard the poisonous narrative circulating in my mind. Maybe I wasn't a good mother. Maybe I just needed to let them go and it was selfish of me to have them. After all, as messed up as I was, it was wrong to want them and desire to be their mother. I imagined I found myself at the crossroads where my biological mother and father must have arrived.

There were moments in the deep, dark pit I found myself, I almost believed those lies. Nevertheless, I kept trying.

I kept fighting for them. I kept fighting for us. I kept fighting so they would have a sober mom with a sound mind in a stable home.

I noticed I possessed a power now I had not experienced before. This gave me hope I could make it through and overcome. Because now, I have Jesus.

WOMEN AND CHILDREN'S TREATMENT CENTER

Despite the many past attempts and failures to get sober and stay clean, I took my youngest daughter and checked into the Women and Children's Treatment Center in Waynoka, Oklahoma.

It was here gospel seeds continued to be planted in my life.

I was beginning to sense somehow everything was different. There was, in fact, a peace and patience present in me which wasn't there before. I started to notice there was a power working through me, enabling me to accomplish things I could not before.

I could stay calm in the midst of correction. I was able to complete things without being led away, confused, or deceived. There was now a rest in my mind. I experienced thoughts which enabled me to stay put and resist spontaneous self-sabotaging suggestions to run restlessly and ruin progress.

There were two pastors who came once a week, gave me a Bible and began teaching me the Word of God. They told me about *Psalm 103:12, which says as far as the east is from the west, so far has God removed my sin from me.*

It was good news for me!

They would pray with me and the other ladies who chose to come. I was very thankful for this experience.

The bus would come get whoever wanted to go to church. I also assisted at the church by waxing the church bus and assisting with funeral dinners, which credited toward the community service points in the steps and mandatory to complete the program.

While at the church one day I sat down on the bench in front of the piano in the sanctuary. Anytime I spot a piano, and it seems appropriate, I go to it and play. I began playing the intro to "Flying Free", the song touched my soul when I was taking lessons as a young girl. It continued to move me and allowed me to express the freedom I so longed for all my life.

Now, I was beginning to taste and experience the true freedom only having a relationship with Jesus can bring.

When I did, Brother John overheard me playing, came into the sanctuary to listen, and later asked me to play a song during the next Sunday morning service. I agreed I would. While playing the song for the congregation, I sensed God's presence, peace, and purpose.

All the while Pastor John was telling me how he used to be an alcoholic before the Lord saved him and called him to preach.

One afternoon after spending time serving at the church, I got back to my room at the center. I felt drawn to my knees, and matter-of-factly prayed, "God, if You are really the God Brother John is saying you are, and you want me to serve you with all my life, then I'm going to need three things only You can do!"

I asked the Lord to deliver me from addiction to drugs and alcohol. I did not want to feel the need for drugs anymore and I knew only He could change it. Second, I asked the Lord to let me know the truth about my adoption. I didn't believe I could really be free unless I knew the truth about where I came from, what happened to me, and who I really am. Finally, I asked the Lord to give me a family which could love each other and serve Him together.

These three things were the desires of my heart and I saw them as the greatest needs of my life.

Waynoka treatment center offered what they called MRT: Moral Recognition Therapy. Recognition therapy is a systematic treatment strategy which seeks to decrease recidivism among juvenile and adult criminal offenders by increasing moral reasoning. There were steps we all worked through at our own pace. We also met together for group sessions. This was of some value.

However, it was the seed of the Word of God spoken to me and people of God placed in my life sharing His love and acceptance meant the most to me and made the most difference. It all spoke to me; God saw me, loved me, and was active in my life. I was very, very thankful.

God's word came alive to me and became a great comfort. I wrote out a verse and taped it on my daughter's and my room door which meant a lot to me.

Consider it pure joy, my brothers and sisters, whenever you face trials of many kinds, because you know that the testing of your faith produces perseverance. Let perseverance finish its work so that you may be mature and complete, not lacking anything. James 1:2-4

Due to God's grace continuously flowing in my life, I was able to complete the four-month program! I was able to show the judge and court a completion certificate.

The process occurring in my life could be paralleled to John 19:30

So when Jesus had received the sour wine, He said, "It is finished!" And bowing His head, He gave up His spirit. John 19:30

DELIVERANCE FROM ADDICTION

*If I go up to the heavens, you are there; if I make
my bed in the depths, you are there. Psalm 139:8
(TPT)*

A special lady stood out to me. I will never forget the woman who worked at Waynoka WCTC by the name of Patsy. She reached out to me for the duration of my treatment stay with gentleness and kindness.

She would say, "He who is in you Barbara is greater than he who is in the world". I realized later she was speaking God's Word to me. It was a verse from the Bible.

The Passion translation puts it like this:

*1 John 4:4 Little children, you can be certain
that you belong to God and have conquered them,
for the One who is living in you is far greater than the
one who is in the world.*

I had been shown and lived through a lot of what the world had to offer. Just because I changed doesn't mean the world did along with me. In fact, at times it seems to be getting worse. And I would soon learn just how tough it could be, being back out there with my new me.

When I left the treatment center in Waynoka, I went through many trials. The only place I knew I could go live was back in Mooreland with my girls' father. He had dropped his petition for divorce, so we were still legally married. There I was again, with nowhere else to go.

The chaos and circumstances I lived in previously produced huge amounts of fear within me. My addiction, the charges and 10-year probation sentence, along with the criminal, immoral allegations presented to me about their father by legal officials and law enforcement all contributed to this fear.

Despite all this, he called to speak to me at the treatment center. He also would come and take me out on what they called a pass, then bring me back to the facility after the pass was over. He always had a persuasive line. He would go on and on and explain how he loved me, how he was sorry, how he had a great deal going where he was making a lot of money and wanted to take care of me and the girls.

I had only recently received Christ. The evidence of His presence and work in my life was fresh. I was still brand new in my faith and salvation.

I realized I had nowhere to go when I left there. I appreciated the rest and provision provided while at the treatment program. However, I needed to be with both my children and create a consistent routine with them. They also needed to spend time together as sisters. I really wanted my girls to have their mom and dad together.

Not knowing what else to do and despite all which happened in the year, I accepted the invitation to get both my daughters and go with their father to Fort Worth, Texas. After spending some time in his family's green-colored house in Mooreland, he took us to live in a home provided by a man he was in business with installing neon lighting around Sonic restaurants. They eventually signed a contract retrofitting stores all over the country. It wasn't long before this plan revealed itself for the mistake it was.

It was good to be out of jail.

It was good having completed my first drug and alcohol treatment and experiencing sobriety. It was great to be back with my girls.

Their dad would tell me he had jobs to do in several different states. He would load up his crew(s), the vans and company vehicles with neon bulbs, equipment, tools, and supplies, and leave for days. He would leave us with food in the house. I didn't have access to a vehicle. Probably best due to my driver's license being suspended from the drug charges. This went on for a few months.

One day he came to the house. While he was standing near the kitchen talking, I smelled a very distinct odor coming from his shirt pocket. Pointing at the bulge in his shirt I asked, "What is it"? He pulled out a baggie, looked at me and said, "It's an ounce of red phosphorus meth".

I was shocked. I was scared.

The next day, I woke up to my children gone and some dope sitting on the kitchen table along with some cocaine and a large bag of syringes. I suddenly felt powerless against it. It was the same cycle. I believed the lies, putting myself back in the relationship with hopes of a different and better outcome only to be rudely awakened to the same; more lies, then defeat and abandonment.

My response to these temptations were extreme anger at being deceived and feeling trapped. I was like a caged wild animal when I felt trapped. To relieve those all-encompassing, overwhelming dark feelings, I would turn to something; chemicals, drugs, alcohol. It was the familiar set up. It was as if it was a game to him to overpower me and control me.

The mental torment which always followed was upon me. Torturous thoughts resurfaced he wanted to get rid of me. I sincerely believed he either wanted me strung out, in prison, or dead. He wasn't going to stop.

I was weary and exhausted from the battle. Sometimes I believed it was easier to simply stop resisting and trying to get away from him. At times, it seemed enticing to fall into a false sense of security denying the truth and escaping reality might bring.

But I knew better now. There is no such thing as escaping reality. Much later it was put to me like this, "Sin will always take you further than you wanted to go, leave you longer than you planned to stay, and cost you more than you ever could possibly pay".

I found out, after some phone calls, he took my girls to his Mom's in Oklahoma without asking me or informing me. I was enraged.

I was frightened even more. I had no way to get to them. I felt trapped, again. I cannot explain why I did the dope. I really didn't want to, but I did.

It was not the same as when I mainlined dope before. It was not me. It did not feel good. I did not enjoy the high. I hated it. I did not understand why I was even doing it. It was almost as if I wasn't even getting high; but more and more frustrated.

I was not darkness anymore. I was something else and this was inconsistent with who I really was now. The struggle went on for a couple weeks. I reminded myself I had made some progress before this, I was now capable of something besides this cycle.

I got word there had been a girl found dead in one of the company vans nearby. There was an investigation. Word was she overdosed, was raped and left there. One of the alleged suspects worked for the company. This brought on increased fear in me.

Not too many days after this surfaced the boss' wife showed up at the door. She straight-forward asked as I opened the door, "Are you ready to leave?" I didn't waste any time replying, "YES". She said get your things together and a man will be by this evening to pick you up.

She explained "I will give this man money to give you and take you to a hotel room in Oklahoma City. I will pay for a room for a week, but you absolutely can NOT contact him." She told me I must not contact him for any reason.

Also, I was not to tell him she was helping me. If I did she was out. She would deny it and not help me anymore. She told me it wasn't right what was going on and she was afraid for me and was why she was helping me 'get out'.

She had inquired in previous brief conversations why I was with such a man. She had told me of some situations she had seen him in, where young girls were held in a room of a house, drugged, and turns were taken by different men, including him to rape them repeatedly. She said she could never see him the same since. She went on, "You are still young and have a chance to get out and make a life for yourself and your girls."

I didn't exactly trust her. However, I agreed. I would get ready and go.

The man showed up in the evening. I packed all the clothes I could in a suitcase and went with him. He drove me from Fort Worth to Oklahoma City in the evening and did exactly what she said he would. I don't remember much being said on the way. When we arrived at the hotel, my room was paid for. I was given a calling card, and some cash. He left.

I really didn't know what to think. I was scared. I didn't know where to go or what to do next. I was glad to be back in Oklahoma, however. I took some of the cash, walked across North West Expressway to a Mexican restaurant, ordered, and ate dinner. Then walked back to the room. I was so tired. I laid back on the pillow and turned on the television. I surfed until I came to a man passionately speaking on a station called TBN. I don't remember his name.

He was sharing about how he used to be addicted to and strung out on drugs. He was describing powerfully how Jesus delivered him, saved, and rescued him from his previous life. Tears began to flow and flow from the corner of my eyes down onto the pillow on each side of my face. It was like my heart started burning

I cried and cried. I cried out to the Lord with a repentant heart. I wept with the fear of God overtaking me. As I listened to the testimony it was a strong reminder the Lord had saved me.

I was His.

He wasn't going to just sit back and allow me to go back to darkness without intervention. Holy Spirit reminded me, as I lay there, who He was.

He was rescuing me.

It was a strong, stern rebuke, yet a still, calm, consistent voice; "Drugs and darkness will lead to death. I am leading you out." Ever since, I have not done drugs or drank alcohol again. Nor have I wanted to. At the writing of this manuscript, I have been clean and sober now for 19 years.

With a strong hand, God delivered me from all desire for alcohol and drugs as I prayed for.

Just like He said He could and would!

―――――――

FINAL ARREST

---

*For you know that your lives were ransomed
once and for all from the empty and futile way of life
handed down from generation to generation. It was
not a ransom payment of silver and gold, which
eventually perishes, but the precious blood of
Christ—who like a spotless, unblemished lamb was
sacrificed for us. 1 Peter 1:18-19 TPT*

I stayed in the hotel room for a few days. I slept mostly. I ate at the complimentary continental breakfast in the lobby in the mornings.

I started thinking.

I began to wonder about the fines he said he was paying on monthly. I walked over to the lobby and used the payphone with the pre-paid card.

I called the courthouse in Woodward county. The court clerk informed me there was a warrant out for my arrest! They issued a warrant for outstanding court costs and failure to pay fines.

Over a thousand dollars had accumulated. I stood there shocked. And, scared all the more. This meant he had not paid even one payment as he said he was. He told me he had been paying it up-to-date since my completion of the treatment program.

I walked back to my room.

Thoughts swirled of how I had been betrayed and "set up" again. The truth is the fines were a direct result from the charges I had plead to and were ultimately my responsibility to pay. I had blindly trusted he was paying them as he said he was.

I was wrong.

Anger mixed with waves of fear settled. What was I going to do? How was I going to take care of this? I did what I had been cautioned and warned not to do by his boss' wife who had got me out and set me up in the room.

I called him.

I wanted to know why. Why had he not paid the fines, and would he pay something to see if they would drop the warrant. The conversation was short. He said he would.

Not long after this conversation a knock came at the hotel room door. It was the police. They arrested me on the warrant. They handcuffed me and put me in the back of the police car.

To the Oklahoma County Jail, I went for booking. My clothes and belongings were left behind in the room. I remained in the Oklahoma County jail (aka money pit) for some days. Small cell, open pod, open community showers, Mexican, Indian, black and white gangs, limited access and time on the payphone were the characteristics sketched in my mind.

When they let us out of our cells there was a lady who stayed close to me. I mean right by my side. She told me she was from Las Vegas and was disabled from being shot in the back running after a drug deal went bad. She had a very unsteady gait. She said the other inmates saw her as weak and a nark. She wanted to stand behind me for protection because I was tall.

It's all about survival.

An officer arrived one day and extradited me back to Woodward county jail. I was back in the same ole familiar jail cell. I was relieved there were no new charges brought against me. However, due to the failure to pay fines the judge could decide to revoke my probation and institute the sentence which had been suspended. It would mean ten years in prison.

I had completed the drug and alcohol program which was part of my sentencing. I had submitted a copy of my completion certificate. I was hoping it would be enough to prove to the court I was at least trying. I knew better than to tell this same judge I had appeared before so many times, I was trusting someone else, my husband whom I had the shady history with, to pay my fines.

I knew it was ultimately my responsibility. By the grace of God, the judge did not revoke my probation. He sentenced me to jail time to pay off my fines.

Since I had been sentenced I applied for trustee. As a trustee I would pay off fines at a higher amount than less than six dollars a day. The judge approved my application. I was now trustee status.

I worked in the jail kitchen making three meals a day for the inmates. Two other ladies and I were allowed out of our cell and in the kitchen by four a.m., making biscuits and gravy from scratch, among many other meals I learned to make.

This incarceration wasn't like the others

I still sensed hope. And indeed, this time in jail proved to be the last!

God's presence was with me still. I would pray to Him. I thanked Him because I did not go to prison and my probation wasn't revoked. He told me He wanted me to surrender completely to Him. He said He wanted me to serve Him with my whole life, He had a great plan for me. He said He hadn't changed His mind.

He called me by name. He called me Barbara. I surrendered.

I told the Lord I don't deserve His love, but I wanted to serve Him. I was thankful for His presence and His protection. I was grateful He had kept me alive and had a plan for the life I had left.

I have gone by the name Barbara ever since. Truth is, Barbara was my original name given to me by my biological mother before my parents relinquished me to foster care. This meant restoration was in the making. God was restoring His original intent and purpose for me.

Colossians 1:20 TPT And by the blood of his cross, everything in heaven and earth is brought back to himself—back to its original intent, restored to innocence again!

I learned later God sometimes changes the name of a person when He transforms them and gets ready to utilize their life for His purposes. Saul to Paul in the New Testament for example.

Considering the sincerity of my confession to live for and serve Jesus, I asked the Lord specifically for a friend when I got out of jail, believing I would more than likely need one.

I was so thankful I was not in Ft. Worth anymore. I missed my daughters terribly.

One day a jailer brought a piece of paper to me with a lady's number on it. It was the same lady who had gotten me out of Ft. Worth to Oklahoma City. The note said to call her collect.

I hesitated.

Because I had not listened to her I felt foolish. But, I called her anyway. She informed me my girls were at their father's parent's house. She went on to say, he had told her and her husband, he was planning to file for divorce while I was in jail so there would be no chance at custody. He had done this before.

And just as she said he would, he did. I was in the jail kitchen helping prepare one of the three meals of the day when I was served the divorce papers. I was required to sign. I stood there just staring at them in somewhat disbelief.

Why I still experienced a degree of shock by the moves he made to control and crush me continues to be a mystery of sorts for me. Fear birthed from cruelty is a tremendously detrimental, paralyzing, manipulative force.

Fear is devastating. People are not meant to be used, owned, enslaved by fear and control. God created people for love, relationship, freedom, and His purposes.

Working as a trustee with the amount of money I had to pay off to the court at the rate I was earning would still take months. I would have no chance at custody.

Besides, then where would I go? Where would I live? What would I do when I get out to support us? Same old trap and predicament.

Once again, she explained she didn't think it was right what was happening to me. She told me she would pay off the rest of my fines, but she would send the money to the court in another person's name, so my husband wouldn't find out or be able to prove it was her.

She said she was truly afraid of him. She said she knew what he was capable of doing.

Wow! What a relief! What a blessing. I could hardly believe she would do this thing. But she did. She paid off the fines.

Court records stated I had served out $1,025.00 in jail already. She sent $1,095.00 in a man's name. Records state the balance in this case of $499.00 was paid. The overpayment of $596.00 was refunded to him (her.)

I consider it the mercy and favor of God.

The day I walked out of the jail, a person who worked there drove me to the Outreach Center in town, a homeless shelter in Woodward.

RESTORED

[ri-stawr, -stohr]

Verb (used with object), re-stored, re-stor-ing.

*To bring back into existence, use, or the like;
reestablish: -- to restore order.*

*2. To bring back to a former, original, or
normal condition, as a building, statue, or painting.*

*3. To bring back to a state of health,
soundness, or vigor*

*4. To put back to a former place, or to a
former position, rank, etc.*

*5. To give back; make return or restitution
of (anything taken away or lost).*

*6. To reproduce or reconstruct (an ancient
building, extinct animal, etc. in the original state.*

HOMELESS SHELTER/CHURCH FAMILY

Therefore, if anyone is in Christ, the new creation has come. The old has gone, the new is here! 2 Corinthians 5:17

The lady who worked at the homeless shelter at the time explained the limit of days to stay was thirty. I had to be actively looking for a job.

I had one change of clothes - jeans with large holes in them, 2 T-shirt's, and the shoes in which I had been arrested.

I left the jail with a white t-shirt which had "INMATE" in block letters painted on the back and another lavender tie-dye t-shirt said, "OKLAHOMA CORRECTIONS". I still have those shirts today and sometimes share my story or lead worship in them as a testimony of how far God can bring someone out of the darkness.

I walked across the street to the first establishment within distance and applied for a job. I was hired at a barbecue restaurant.

I began waitressing.

After explaining some of my situation to the owner, he took me to the tack shop in town and bought me two pairs of rocky mountain jeans and provided the business shirts to wear so I would be in uniform for work. I enjoyed waitressing. I love people and serving. I was out of jail, sober, and saved!

I was thankful!

Soon after arriving at the shelter, I met a lady who was volunteering her time in the clothing room, folding and organizing donated clothes. She reached out to me with the kindness and gentleness of Jesus. She handed me a Christian CD by Stephen Curtis Chapman and invited me to her church. She exhibited patience and prayed often with me. She was the friend I had prayed for! She became very special to me and my girls.

Lana, the friend and mentor I prayed God would send during my final incarceration, whom I met at the homeless shelter.

Father provided not only fun and friendship in Lana, but she also was a kind of mentor, and offered discipleship for me as I was truly beginning my sold-out, committed, surrendered walk with God. It was a tremendous honor, some years later, to be a bridesmaid in her wedding.

My friend Lana picked me up at the Homeless Outreach Center and drove us to church one Sunday morning. I'll never forget sensing the glory of God when I walked into the sanctuary for the first time! I was so thankful to be in the midst of these people and the presence of God! I did what they suggested to become what they considered a member.

I went forward to the front of the sanctuary where Pastor Russell Duck was standing at the closing of a Sunday morning service. I expressed my desire to become a part of the church.

First Baptist Church in Woodward, Oklahoma became a family to me and my girls as I made the transition from the kingdom of darkness into the kingdom of light. The people of this church embraced me and taught me what it means to love.

My girls and I for First Baptist Woodward, Oklahoma church directory.

When I was lost, on the street, using drugs, drinking, and running, life was all about myself. Life was, how I can survive and serve myself, feed an addiction, and run from pain, reality, and responsibility.

Now it's all about Jesus and how I can serve Him and others.

This church modeled this type love for me. My heart overflows with thankfulness and love as I think about all the beautiful people and families we walked beside in life with for over a decade. Back then, as I walked the halls of the church, excited to attend everything

I could which they offered, I sensed redemption as I would pass police officers and other various officials of the community in the house of God.

One day, one of the Pastors stopped and point blank asked me, "So what's your story"?

This question began and forged a dialogue which created a friendship very meaningful and significant, not only in my spiritual growth but biblical counseling and mentoring helped me to learn and heal. For the next ten years Pastor Tony Barros proved to be, and I trusted him to be, my pastor, counselor, teacher, and friend. Eventually, he became a partner in ministry as well. We often discussed what the Lord was doing in my life, how He was speaking and leading. During one discipleship counseling session, Pastor Tony prophesied I would become a nurse.

Teaching ladies Sunday School class First Baptist Woodward

Similarly, Sarai in the old testament, God spoke to her saying she would have a son and she laughed because she thought she was too old. I thought for a second and then replied, "There was no way I could become a nurse. I have been convicted of multiple felonies and a drug charge to boot!" Being a nurse wasn't even on the radar and even if it had been, I believed it was an impossibility for me with my situation and background.

He also anointed me with oil and prayed for healing one day after I told him of a surgery I was facing to take care of some lower digestive tract issues. I have no way of knowing for sure, but I suspect these ailments came about after all the drugs and alcohol I consumed and injected, while going long periods of time without eating and sleeping.

I arrived at the appointment, was prepped for surgery, and given sedation. When I came to on the table the physician explained to me when they went in to perform the surgery the issue had already been removed! There was no need for surgery! I was healed physically from the specific ailment.

The church would hold Wednesday evening meals with various activities, ministries and studies. One Wednesday evening, not long after attending the church, I was standing in the meal line. After a few moments of wondering, I acknowledged a lady standing next to me in line. I recognized her. It was the lady who led me to Christ in jail! I was so excited.

I had not seen her since she had come to the jail, about two years prior. I was able to tell Ms. Sharon Jackson the difference she made in my life when she came to the jail those years earlier. I shared with her I had prayed for Jesus to come into my life and was saved the day she came to the jail. I told her I bowed my head and prayed after she went down to the next cell.

Ever since, we have a special friendship and bond. It was especially comforting to see her and served as a confirmation I was in the right place. God was at work in my life, leading me in His direction.

What a gift. What a connection

During this same time, while staying at the homeless shelter outreach, I noticed my husband's rag-top Cadillac circling the building in the evenings. I continued to experience fear of him and what I knew he had the capacity to do. I didn't want to see him. I didn't want him to know I was out of jail.

I wanted to work long enough to save up money for a retainer toward an attorney in order to have a fighting chance for custody of my girls. I had been served with divorce papers while in jail and it was still pending.

If possible, I also wanted to find a small home and save enough for a deposit and first month's rent. If I could get an attorney and home, then I could tell the judge I was stable enough to have my girls when we went to court to settle the divorce. I thought I could possibly be awarded child support, which could help pay the bills once the girls and I were together.

He began calling the community phone in the living room at the homeless shelter asking to talk to me. I refused his calls. One day out front, as I walked across the street to work at my waitressing job, he pulled up in his car and rolled down the window. He handed me a check for a large amount and told me he loved me.

Reluctantly, I took the check.

I took the money and retained an attorney. I also paid the deposit and first month's rent on a small three-bedroom home across town, right next to the train tracks. I established a landline phone, so I could stay in communication with my girls. I got used to the sound of the train going by.

It recently reminded me if I was on the land-line phone with someone, they would ask, "What is the noise in the background?"

"It's just the train going by," I would respond. The conversation would have to pause until the train passed. Sometimes it was just easier to end the call rather than yell at the caller.

My babies and I at the rent house with the loud trains.

It wasn't long after moving in, the divorce was finalized. The decree stated we shared joint custody placing me as primary custodial parent. I finally had what I had fought so hard for - my babies!

However, I had no car and was granted a little over two hundred dollars a month in child support. It was not enough to even pay rent. I applied and was given an allotment of monthly food stamps. I couldn't afford or find child care to continue working. But I had a home, my girls, a church, and a love for my Savior.

I was tremendously thankful.

My friend Lana would pick me and my girls up from the rent house and take us to church. Lana had also shared with me about a ministry called, "Freedom in Christ" by Neil T. Anderson. She offered me a workbook as preparation to a session which would take place later. I read over the information.

She, a lady friend named Jean, and I met in a small town nearby at a lodge style cabin called, "High Adventure". Jean was to be the prayer warrior who remained present in the room during the sessions. Lana led through what they termed the "steps to freedom in Christ". What I remember most is what consisted of confessing and renouncing any and all involvement or open doors into sin and occult, knowingly or unknowingly. It took hours. It was a full day.

I did it. I was very careful to be completely honest through the entire process. I was transparent about sins I had committed and immoral activities I'd been involved in, and then renounced all belief in, dependency on, or ties with these things. We prayed thorough prayers making sure I had not missed or skipped over an area.

The steps are:
1. Counterfeit vs. Real

2. Deception vs. Truth

3. Bitterness vs. Forgiveness

4. Rebellion vs Submission

5. Pride vs. Humility

6. Bondage vs. Freedom

7. Curses vs. Blessings

Overall, I believe it was a spiritually cleansing and freeing opportunity. I would order and utilize those same workbooks with other women who came to my home years later. And, I would simply send the workbook to others in the mail.

With what little money I had I decided to rent a piano from a local music store. I thought God might be wanting me to take up my playing once again. I determined I wouldn't know for sure unless I sat down and began to practice.

Playing had been something I enjoyed and served as an outlet to expression when I was growing up and a symbol of freedom when I would see one throughout my journey.

I played "Flying Free", the song with the bird in flight on the front cover over and over. In Christ I continued tasting and experiencing more and more of the freedom I had only dreamed about years ago.

I joined the choir at my church. Not long after I joined and began rehearsing regularly I was invited to sing a solo part in a large production. The song I was asked to perform was so perfect and fitting as to how I felt and the cry of my heart at this time. I was nervous but when I looked out into the audience and saw my mom it calmed me. It was a healing moment.

With the full choir behind me, I sang the words to the first stanza as best as I could while fighting back tears:

I will never be the same again,

I can never return, I've closed the door.

I will walk the path, I'll run the race

And I will never be the same again.

Fall like fire, soak like rain,

Flow like mighty waters, again and again.

Sweep away the darkness, burn away the chaff,

And let the flame burn to glorify Your name.

There are higher heights, there are deeper seas,

Whatever you need to do, Lord do in me.

The Glory of God fills my life,

And I will never be the same again.

"I Will Never Be The Same Again" (excerpt)

~Darlene Zschech, Hillsong

My girls began Sunday school classes. From this time until their teenage years they were involved in classes, bible drill, Kids Kamp every summer, biblical play productions, then later Falls Creek, Awana's, and youth group at our church. Later they would attend Woodward Christian Academy for some years of their education.

I wanted us to know Jesus and grow in Him together as a family. This is one of the three things I asked God for after my salvation. A family which could love God and serve Him together.

BIOLOGICAL INFORMATION

---

*Jesus said, "If you hold to my teaching, you are
really my disciples. Then you will know the truth,
and the truth will set you free. John 8:32*

I completed my first bible study while living at the new house with the loud trains. The ladies at the church would all meet one day a week and we would discuss the topics of the week, share the answers to our questions, and watch a video.

I absolutely loved it! I was so hungry for the Word of God, for truth.

The first study I completed was called, "Breaking Free" by Beth Moore. It could not have been more appropriate and applicable to my life. The subtitle read: "Making Liberty in Christ a Reality in Life".

The videos and workbook led through a study of scriptures to discover the transforming power of Christian freedom. It taught what God intends for me to; know God and believe Him, glorify God, find satisfaction in God, experience God's peace, and enjoy His presence.

It showed how to remove obstacles which hinder relationships. It helped me identify spiritual strongholds in my life. It had lessons about generational curses and generational sins passed down from fathers, mothers, and ancestors.

Another one of the three things I had asked from God early in my Christian life, was to learn the truth about my adoption. I sensed there were spiritual issues affecting my life which were a direct result of my biological beginnings.

I didn't think I could really be free unless I knew the truth about the circumstances surrounding where, who, and what type of situation I came from. Not only did I smoke my last cigarette while going through this study, also through a series of events, I was led to the state capital in Oklahoma City where I learned of an adoption registry.

I filled out a lengthy application requesting all non-identifiable information pertaining to my adoption. Not long after applying I received the information in the mail.

On June 1, 2000, I sat down to complete my daily bible study and prayed over the letter before opening it. I was excited and a bit nervous. I had wondered and waited most my life to learn something about my biological situation and now I had at least a piece of the puzzle right before me.

I prayed, "God, thank you for this day. I prayed specifically for information about my biological family and myself and you have answered my prayer. Whatever information is in this envelope I will accept it and thank you for it."

The opening cover letter stated the data and documents included were based on information currently available to them in the DHS adoption files. It further stated, "We have provided this information to the best of our knowledge and belief and consider it is true, correct, and complete." I read through the confidential materials from their microfilm files.

The second page was Child Health and Family History:
Barbara Renee' Saunders. Place of birth was Tulsa.
It listed a record of immunizations I had received from August of 1975 through January of 1976.
Section *"Traumas, accidents, or illnesses requiring medical treatment or hospitalization from first years of life to present"*:
January, 1974 (3 months old) Fractured arm
01/20/1976 Dry skin, small umbilical hernia
03/24/1976 Ear infection
05/05/1976 Fever, otitis media, head cold
05/19/1976 Otitis media resolved
10/25/1976 Fever, Viral throat infection
01/24/1977 Burn from heater-2nd degree burns L. hand and L knee
(Entered Foster Care)--
04/20/1977 Dental check up
04/21/1977 Well Child

Under *"Psychological history and results of available psychological examinations"*:
IQ 106, within average or above. Strengths in tasks involving memory and eye-hand coordination.

Section II. SOCIAL HISTORY: Information regarding past and existing relationships among child and siblings:

Two brothers, one a year older and second one two years older.

Extended family known to have been involved with the child:

Step-maternal grandmother, paternal grandfather, and maternal grandmother.

Circumstances leading to child's removal from home of birth family (as judged by worker):

Severe environmental deprivation in home. Children removed at parent's request. Birth mother not capable of taking care of children, suffers from mental disabilities. Birth father has a drinking problem and is unable to maintain employment.

Number of known placements to date:

One foster home, then adoptive family.

Describe the child's personality, talents, preferences:

Cute expressions, mimics others behavior, plays well alone, independent. Likes to dance with music.

Separate page listing information pertaining to biological Father:

Was an alcoholic. It stated he had been in and out of treatment, but never completed treatment. He was born in Alabama, had dark hair and dark eyes and was 6'2" in height. It stated he had been in the Navy National Guard for 13 years and was given general discharge for bad conduct and going AWOL due to drinking problem. It also said he had a hard time maintaining employment. He had graduated high school and had some history as an automotive and painting contractor.

Separate page listing information pertaining to my Biological Mother:

Born in Oklahoma is 5'3" in height, weighed 250 lbs., green eyes, and has light brown hair color.

"Health and Medical History":

"Mentally Retarded. Was described as very nervous. Attended group counseling for daily living skills". Under Significant emotional/behavioral history it stated: "Received SSI benefits for her disability. Described as a "slow learner" and did not know how to handle money. IQ 36, but actually functioned on a higher level. Highest level of formal education completed 9th grade. Employment History listed was "Food Service".

Four pages attached for information concerning Maternal and Paternal Grandmothers and Grandfathers. And even though it stated, "Extended family known to have been involved with the child", all the blanks for Step-maternal grandmother, paternal grandfather, and maternal grandmother were empty.

Some of the information was shocking to me. Some of it was painful. Finding out I had two biological brothers was surprising and exciting!

Mostly, I was so grateful to God to get this information. It set me free from years of not knowing. The Bible says in *John 8:32*

> *You shall know the truth and the truth shall set you free.*

And indeed, it did just what it said!

The truth about the gospel, the truth about your life, the truth about who you are in Christ and truly the things which set us all free. God sees the whole picture. He knows the beginning and the end, including everything in between.

His perspective is what I desire. I wanted to know these things long before I obtained them. However, God's timing is perfect. He led me to and revealed the pieces of the puzzle of my life when He knew I was ready.

Freedom is the goal; not despair. Without the truth, however, there is no freedom. I was now saved, sober, and in a position to receive the truth and continue healing.

The opening letter I received also stated:

"Effective November 1, 1997 (not long prior to my salvation in 1998), the Department of Human Services established a Confidential Intermediary Search Program for eligible individuals separated from birth family members through adoption or termination of parental rights. In order to take advantage of this program, you must be on the Mutual Consent Voluntary Reunion Registry for six months."

It also listed the name of a lady who held the position of "Programs Field Representative of the Adoptions Section of Children and Family Services". There was a contact number.

I waited. I prayed. I continued to grow in Christ. I took time to process all the information I had learned.

I called my mom and shared with her the information. She listened. She was understanding and supportive.

Jesus was setting me free. His word was transforming my mind and teaching me His perspectives. He was answering prayers and I loved my new life in Him.

However, some things didn't just go away.

My daughters' father went from circling the homeless shelter, where I stayed previously, to circling the home where I now rented and lived. The fear this produced is hard to describe. It broke me down over time.

It was like, with each next step of truth led to more freedom and knowing who I really am, as well as understanding how much God really loved me and was for me, there was also an opposite force present and at work as well. "Don't ever think you're going to become completely free. You don't deserve to be free. How dare you even try and leave. You're just a whore. You're nothing. You will be a slave and held down forever. You'll never fully get out." It is a dangerous narrative to entertain and I was fighting it with everything I had.

He knocked on the door one day while I was there alone. He came in, said some things, and began kissing me, pushing me on the bed, pulling my pants down. It took place very quickly. I didn't fight. He finished, got up, walked into my bathroom while saying a few words. He then sat down on the couch for a few minutes, then left.

I felt sad. I felt defeated.

I got pregnant. I told God I would never have another abortion. I resolved to keep my promise to God and trust Him with this pregnancy and child. I notified him I was pregnant. Then their father began calling on a regular basis.

One day he told of how he had picked up a hitchhiker, began witnessing to him about Jesus. He said he was "so moved by the Holy Spirit he received Christ and cast the demon out of him right through the windshield." He said he loved me and wanted to change and be a family. He asked if he could come over and see the girls and have Thanksgiving together. Reluctantly, I agreed.

Now pregnant, their dad would say, and I reasoned as well also in my weakness and need, God must want us together. Perhaps God could really be reconciling our marriage and family? He kept asking me to marry him again.

126

I shared with my pastor I was pregnant.

I was told since I was not married and now pregnant, and because by this time I was not only singing in the choir, but I had been appointed as a choir officer in the Alto section, I was asked and required to stand before the church assembly and publicly repent, as well as voluntarily step down from choir leadership.

I was also told because their father wasn't an actual member of the church, the church couldn't ask him to submit to the same public repentance. Furthermore, I was asked to inform him if he came to church with me it would be evidence of on-going sin and I could be asked to leave the church.

This ranks up there as one of the most devastating and I would say humbling, more accurately described as humiliating things which happened to me.

My heart broke. I knew there was a decision for me to make.

It is still a toss-up as to which act was more degrading and shame-filled; getting over-taken and taken advantage of again by the man you are desperately seeking freedom from or being asked to publicly display yourself as a sexually immoral sinner before an entire congregation of people you have come to love and appreciate.

I prayed. I cried. I decided to do what my leaders and pastor asked me to do. I submitted to their authority.

At the time, it was more important to me and very crucial to continue to grow in my walk with God among the church then to leave. I drank the cup of humility. On a Sunday I stood before the people of my church. The pastor spoke for me.

I said nothing. Only nodded my head in agreement as he spoke about my coming forward as repentance, forgiveness, and restoration. As I took a solid stance before the church and as words were being spoken about my sin, I gazed just above the people toward the top of the sanctuary.

I saw the presence of the Holy Spirit. I sensed the comforting presence of the Holy Spirit as He held me and ministered to me in those moments. It was if all the people were gone and it was only Holy Spirit and me.

I was strengthened through the shame. I was being held by God.

After the service some of the people of my church walked up to me. Some were crying. Most were compassionate and understanding. Some hugged me, placed their hands on me, and prayed for me and my baby right there.

The next weeks and months there were phone calls, emails, and conversations with people who expressed their apologies. They told me they felt what I was asked to do was not right. It was "legalistic and wrong". They reminded me of the account in the bible of the women caught in adultery. He without sin cast the first stone and so on. I was appreciative of their support and kindness reaching out to me. However, I was careful not to speak against my leaders. They did what they thought was best and biblical. It was very difficult for all. I did not want to be the cause of any division. I truly loved all my church family and it grieved me deeply to be in the situation.

I believed by handling it the way I did and how it was asked of me, it created ground for forgiveness and healing instead of grumbling and bitterness. It wasn't about who was right or wrong. For me, it was about continuing to remain and grow in Christ.

You see, as broken as I was, it was still what I wanted most, and I was willing to do the hard things. I also continued to desire a healthy family who could love God and one another and could serve Christ together.

I gave birth to my third beautiful baby girl. I love her with all my heart! I'm so thankful from the time she was born she was pure joy and delight and her momma was saved and sober.

My third beautiful girl, Brook.

A few months later, I married their father again. He rented us all a home in Woodward for some time, but eventually bought a home back in Mooreland attached to the five acres where his family's other home was located and where we lived before. He utilized the building there for his office when he was in town.

About a year after receiving the non-identifiable information about my biological family, I was watching a children's movie entitled, "Joseph, King of Dreams" with my girls. It was a cartoon rendition taken from Genesis chapter 45. It is the story of Joseph sold into slavery by his brothers, being falsely accused and put into prison, then raised up, second only to Pharaoh.

After 26 years God reunited Joseph with his father and brothers. As I was watching this depicted I began to pray, "God, You're the same yesterday, today, and forever. What You did for Joseph, maybe You could do for me?" By this time, I had my unidentifiable information for about a year. I called the number and name on the paperwork expressing a desire for them to search for my biological family. They stated for a fee they would find my family and if they agreed to meet, we could be reunited!

RECONCILIATION

*Never doubt God's mighty power to work in you
and accomplish all this. He will achieve infinitely
more than your greatest request, your most
unbelievable dream, and exceed your wildest
imagination! He will outdo them all, for his
miraculous power constantly energizes you.*

Ephesians 3:20 TPT

In a relatively short period of time they found all the members of my biological family. My middle brother, Robert (Bobby) was in an Oklahoma prison when they found him. A case worker went there to tell him his biological sister was looking for him, and I would like to meet him. He sent me a picture of himself and a letter in the mail! In the picture he wore jail oranges holding a C.A.S.A completion certificate. The overwhelming joy of laying my eyes on a picture of him overshadowed any shade of orange he was wearing and why.

After he was released some time later, we were able to meet. He shared with me he was adopted by a family and grew up in Chickasha, Oklahoma. It was shocking how much we looked alike and how much he favored our biological father in appearance. Being adopted I wondered if I looked like my biological family members. It is truly an amazing gift to lay eyes on them and talk to them 26 years later.

Thank you, God!

My biological brother Robert (Bobby) and me, visiting day at First Step Men's Recovery Program Oklahoma City.

I received a phone number for my oldest brother. I was told his name was Frazier Esten. After calling and having a conversation with him, he shared when he was adopted he chose the name John asking to be named after the man in the Bible who wore different clothes, ate locusts, and was baptized in the river. We spoke on the phone first and then arranged a visit.

I drove to Enid, Oklahoma a little over an hour from Mooreland where I lived at the time, to meet my oldest brother John. What a gift! He lives with a disability similar to our biological mother yet higher functioning. At the time of our reunion, he lived in an independent living/group home type condo for people with his type disability.

The day I reunited with my biological brother John in Enid, Oklahoma after being separated for 26 years. December 21, 2001

After meeting his adoptive parents some time later, they shared more of John's story with me. His adoption was a result of a Channel 5 News program known as "Wednesday's Child". Wednesday's Child is a televised feature which helps recruit adoptive families who can provide permanent and loving homes for children in the foster care system.

Royce and Ruby Jordan, a couple who would become John's adopted parents spotted him on television as they were watching the news one day. Sure enough, a special day not long after this broadcast they brought my brother John to Buffalo, Oklahoma. John remembers coming to Buffalo in a helicopter accompanied by Jack Bowen, a channel 5 news anchor, and landing near the park. He was then greeted by a gathering of is new forever family. The Jordan's and many others in the town welcomed him graciously.

It wasn't long after meeting my brother John and learning some of his adoption story, I was attending the annual Evangelism Conference held at First Baptist Church in Moore, Oklahoma. Guess who just so happened to be there? Jack Bowen! I introduced myself. I shared I had just reunited with my biological family after twenty-six years.

I mentioned I knew it had been a long time, but did he happen to remember a Wednesday's Child named John adopted to a family in Buffalo, Oklahoma? He smiled and immediately said, "Actually, I do!" We continued to have a nice visit. He was gracious enough to have our picture taken together. He told me I could show my brother and his family. I knew they would be excited I ran into him so soon after our reuniting.

Running into Jack Bowen Channel 9 News anchor soon after reuniting with my brother John at the annual Evangelism Conference at First Baptist Church Moore, Oklahoma. Bowen covered John's adoption story on "Wednesday's Child."

Who is this God we serve? This God who cares enough to orchestrate such kind appointments. He is in the tiniest details of life. The same day after meeting my oldest biological brother John, I went to Sand Springs, near Tulsa, Oklahoma where I was born, to meet my biological parents who were still together. This surprised me. It is challenging to find the words to describe the feelings I was experiencing in my anticipation to meet them.

I was excited. It was surreal. It was a dream come true and a prayer answered.

Pulling up to the address I was given in Sand Springs, Oklahoma, I got out of the truck and walked up to the door of the tiny shack-like place.

I knocked.

A tall, very thin man answered. It was him! It was my biological father. He wore painter pants, a thin shirt, and combat boots. He greeted me with a wide smile. I noticed he had only one remaining tooth. I introduced myself. He said his name was James.

I could hear a voice coming from inside the door, "Barbara, is that you?" He invited me inside. I could then immediately see my biological mother sitting on the edge of a bed which was positioned in the front room, as I stepped inside. There were roaches crawling all over everything; the walls, the tables, the floor. There was a foul smell I can't put a name to, and only patches of carpet with holes exposing portions of the subflooring. Webs of dust hanging almost as low as the dirty, stained chairs.

There, we all three were, looking at each other. We all appeared to be nervous, not exactly knowing what to say or how to respond. There was a deeper sense of destiny, however.

After what seemed like more than just a few minutes of looking at each other, my father began to weep. As he wept he looked at Vonda, my mother, then back at me.

Through the tears he looked at me and said, "Forgive us. Please forgive us". Vonda then said, "Yes, forgive us". "DONE," I responded. I sat down beside Vonda. She was wrapped in a blanket of sorts and as I looked at her hands, I soon put it together her fingers were stained with feces.

She began explaining, "When you were a year old, we were living in the basement of a building with four other families, no running water." She went on to say at some point she and James, "Called welfare to get help, but when they saw the conditions we were living in they, took my brothers and I, gave us new names, and adopted us out".

She continued to say just about two months prior to us all meeting, a friend of hers invited her to a church in Tulsa. She decided to go. She heard the truth, the gospel - Jesus can save you, forgive your sins, heal you, and change your life. She said she went forward and gave her life to the Lord.

She went on to say, as she was counseling with the lady at the front of the church at the time of her salvation, the one thing she said she wanted from God was to meet her daughter. God is so wonderful.

The lady that prayed with and led my biological mom, Vonda to Christ at the front of her church just prior to us reuniting.

Two months later, after twenty-six years, there we were. They were meeting their daughter and I was, meeting my biological parents. Not only did God reconcile me to my biological family and my daughters, but I'm now a part of an eternal family.

The day I reunited with my biological parents after 26 years of separation in Sand Springs, Oklahoma December 21, 2001. What a Christmas gift!

Ephesians 1:3-14: Praise be to the God and Father of our Lord Jesus Christ, who has blessed us in the heavenly realms with every spiritual blessing in Christ. For he chose us in him before the creation of the world to be holy and blameless in his sight. In love he predestined us for adoption to sonship through Jesus Christ, in accordance with his pleasure and will--to the praise of his glorious grace, which he has freely given us in the One he loves. In him we have redemption through his blood, the forgiveness of sins, in accordance with the riches of God's grace that he lavished on us. With all wisdom and understanding, he made known to us the mystery of his will according to his good pleasure.

What is even better, we all must be adopted into God's family. No one can come on their own. There is no other way. We all must go through the blood of Jesus.

Toward the end of our initial reunion visit, James, my biological father, was standing near a window leaning into the light. He lingered there, as he seemed to be looking for something. He continued to thumb through the contents of his wallet over and over. Soon he smiled and said, "Found it!"

He pulled out an old folded, tattered and somewhat torn picture. With it in his hand he held it out to me explaining, "This is you and your brothers sitting on my lap at the welfare office right before they took all of you". I took some steps closer to him. I could hardly believe it. There I was as a little girl, sitting on his lap with both my brothers. He had saved the picture all those years, over two and a half decades.

When our visit ended for the day, I took the picture to the nearest Wal-Mart. I asked the photo department to do their best restoring the image and having it enlarged. The result was a 11x13 frame of this treasure mounted above the desk in my home office. It was a daily reminder of how gracious and good Father God really is to have made a way to meet my biological parents.

The photo also represents a new discovery; not only am I loved by my Heavenly Father, but I also now had evidence the man who gave birth to me, kept me close to him all those years, even if it was only in the form of a picture. The picture was a special gift and another piece to a broken and scattered puzzle.

James, my biological father, shared later some of the names and numbers for extended family on his side. He offered a number for his father, which would be my grandfather and his sisters, my aunts. I called and spoke with my grandfather James White, Sr., over the telephone. He shared with me how he met me when I was very little. He lived in Cottondale, Alabama, which is the state my biological father James Jr. was from originally.

My brothers and I sitting on our biological father's lap at the child welfare office the day we were all relinquished and separated. My biological father, James kept this picture in his wallet for 26 years and presented it to me when we reunited.

He sent me a picture of himself. In the picture, he had a suede leather coat with what looked like Native American attire and beads. I was told by James Jr. and James Sr. our blood was "French Indian" and it was also mentioned we are a percentage from one of the Osage tribes. It was so exciting to be able to speak with my biological grandfather. He passed away not long after we spoke.

I also called the numbers given to me for my aunts, James' sisters. I spoke with a woman named Martha who confirmed she was my biological father's sister, my aunt. She shared with me more details from her perspective and memory.

She calmly told of her recollection after welfare services found us all living in the basement in what they considered a severely deprived environment. They then took my brothers and I into custody and put us into foster homes. However, she said welfare attempted to work with my biological parents and did place me and my brothers back with them for a time as an attempt to keep us all together.

They managed to move into an apartment just down the hall from my aunt. She reluctantly, yet honestly revealed when I was placed back with my biological parents, she could hear the abuse taking place. She said night after night, she heard when I was beat against the walls over and over. She said she heard when I was yelled and screamed at to "SHUT UP" and "STOP CRYING" again and again.

She began expressing her sincere apologies to me. Shocked I asked, "What for, you didn't do it". She humbly responded, "Because I heard what was going on and I did nothing for a long time". She went on to say she couldn't stand to know and hear any more, so she finally was the one who called the police and made the report of the ongoing abuse. It was soon after this my biological parents then agreed to make the decision to relinquish custody of us permanently.

Again, this information was difficult and painful to hear. However painful it was, it didn't compare to missing portions of my life. These critical details fell into place and painted a more complete picture, where there had been nothing but questions and unknowns before.

I had been a scared little girl, who had shut down emotionally. I was unable to cry and terrified to be touched. I was convinced, at one time, I was unlovable. I believed I was undeserving of love, and incapable of accepting love and affection.

This now made sense for me why I had suffered so much. I thanked her for being honest and expressed the desire to hopefully meet her one day.

After this, James and Vonda came to visit my home. James even painted the entire outside of my home and a few rooms inside as we were moving back to Mooreland, Oklahoma from Woodward during this time. This was a nice gift.

I rented a hotel room for them to stay while in town and they attended church with me for the week. I took them to Sunday School with me and was excited to introduce them to my class and church family.

During the week there was discussion, after I offered to help them move closer, so we could get to know one another more. I could also offer them some help. I had noticed their living conditions were less than safe or healthy. Even so, they decided after the week, they would go back to their home in Sand Springs. They said they missed their litter of kittens and cats.

I'm thankful for the week and the time I was able to spend with them both. A couple years after meeting my biological parents, I received a phone call James had passed away one morning while waiting for the home delivery of oxygen. He was diagnosed and had been living with emphysema.

Their church helped Vonda arrange for his funeral in Sand Springs. I attended the funeral. I stood before the handful of folks in attendance. I felt led to share some of our family's story of separation and reconciliation.

I sang Amazing Grace. I wept my way through the words and notes of the song. My body literally shook as I sang. While singing I was contemplating the reality of all God had done.

I am sad I only had a couple years to get to know James. I am also tremendously thankful for the time we did have, and I was able to meet my biological father before he passed away.

Truly amazing grace.

I was once again reminded, soon after my salvation in jail I asked the Lord for those three things, the desires of my heart, things only He could do. He has been faithful to accomplish all three, and so much more. In His time, His way.

At times I believed God was doing one thing and yet, time would prove what I was experiencing was simply seasonal or for a purpose. It has proven to be a process to gain Fathers perspective. However, He has answered my prayers.

Father continues to redeem and restore my life. He has redeemed all the pain from things which happened to me and poor decisions I made as a result. My life is now an offering.

As Pastor Tony used to say, the good, the bad, the ugly for His glory to help others know Him. This is all I really desire now. In all I do and say I want my life to point to Jesus. I want to know and serve Him. I want to go wherever He leads.

FREE AT LAST MINISTRIES, INC.

It is for freedom that Christ has set us free.
Stand firm, then, and do not let yourselves be
burdened again by a yoke of slavery. Galatians 5:1

I was praying for direction. Praying about what I should do with my life now which Jesus was leading. I wanted to serve my Lord. I wanted to receive and utilize the salvation and gifts He had given me for His glory, so others could come to know Him.

Father God confirmed during this time, He desired and delighted in my worship through music and singing. However, He also had another avenue of freedom, expression, and purpose in mind. He was going to restore my voice and speak through me.

I went through a short season of questioning if, as a women, I was to be speaking and proclaiming His word publicly as I was. I had just spoke for a large event in Oklahoma City at the peak of this questioning.

Afterwards, I knelt down to my knees in prayer by my bed in the hotel room asking God if I was doing His will with my speaking or if it was just something I set out to do. I asked Him to please show me the truth. I only wanted to do His will for my life.

When I set out for home I came upon a garage sale sign. I normally didn't frequent garage sales. However, I was drawn to this one. I was not in a huge hurry to get back home so I turned down the road where the arrow was pointing to check it out.

I stepped out of my jeep and began walking up the long drive way to the garage sale. That's when I spotted it. I couldn't believe it. I shook my head in amazement. "No way," I thought.

At the corner of the drive there stood a pulpit! There was a sign of $60 in black marker taped to the top. I walked over to a lady seemingly in charge and offered $30 for it, as I didn't have enough for the asking price.

The pulpit God used from a garage sale to lay to rest questions I was having about being a lady public communicator and to confirm my call to an evangelistic speaking journey.

She responded, "Well, actually this is a multi-family garage sale. The lady who owns that left and said if someone makes an offer on the pulpit, just give it to them!" Wait what?! Mind blown.

God had shown me! It was His answer to reassure me I was obeying Him and being led by Him. I loaded it up in the jeep took it home, sanded and re-stained it. It sat in my living room for years as a reminder He had called me, a women, to speak, share, and publicly proclaim. I would prepare the messages I was called on to share standing at that pulpit.

The first event I was invited to speak at was a Gideon Pastors banquet held at my church. I experienced a bit of nervousness. However, I did not want to utilize notes. Once I began speaking though, it was as if the Holy Spirit took over.

I knew as I was sharing, I was doing exactly what God had called me to do. His presence was so powerful and the response of the people so warm and encouraging. Sharing my story began what has now become an almost twenty-year long ministry.

It has been healing to not only share portions of my life in 10-20 minute and hour-long increments, but the Word of God as it pertained and actively applied to each and every season of my life since.

More recently after sharing my story a gentleman came to me and said, "When you share your story, it is prophetic." I have also learned at least one meaning of the word testimony is literally, "To do again".

By sharing my testimony publicly, it isn't as much about me sharing facts about my life, as it is the desire for God to "Do it again". And He does this by setting free someone else's life who is present when I share or when they read my story.

As you read, it is my wish you are touched and grow to understand Jesus died to save and set us all free. May you surrender and call upon His name now.

John 1:12 Yet to all who did receive Him, to
those who believed in His name, He gave the right to
become children of God--

I also traveled and shared testimony for not only Gideon Pastors banquets but Gideon State Conventions, as well. I traveled to Atlanta, Georgia to speak at the Gideon International Convention. While speaking there my testimony was being translated into at least six different languages as I spoke. It was an incredible and humbling thought to look out and see the different translators in the booths across the room.

Gideon International Convention, Atlanta, Georgia. Sharing my testimony that was translated into six languages during this event

Around 2007 I was scheduled to speak at a Mississippi State Gideon Convention in Tupelo. Arriving at Will Rogers World Airport in Oklahoma City I barely missed the flight by 10 minutes. There had been a time change without my knowledge.

I was sad on the two-in-a-half hour drive back home. Sad because I missed such a great opportunity at the Convention, but it had also been arranged for me to interview live at the American Family Radio studio the next day.

Turns out I could still interview. However, it would be live over a phone connection. I sat in my office at home responding to their leads and questions regarding my life story. They had listeners call in if they had questions. I remember two callers especially. A man caller and a lady caller.

The lady caller shared she felt as if God was calling her to prison ministry. She explained somewhat of a struggle with it expressing "But I haven't been through anything like you. What would I have to offer them?"

I encouraged her to consider what brought her to the cross, what brought her to repentance and faith in Jesus? All of us who know Jesus have a story of transformation. We were one person behaving one way before Christ, then somehow, somewhere, some way we came to know Him, and now we are a completely new, all together new creation. The specifics, behaviors, details may not be the same or they may seem totally different, but we all must come to Christ knowing on some level our depravity is due to our own sin and rebellion, creating separation from God.

Building bridges to others having common experiences and like circumstances is powerful. However, it is also the pure love of God and compassion shed abroad in our hearts through knowing and walking with him which draws people and leads them to longing for a relationship with Him.

People come to where love is. Both stand points expressed from one person to another can make the difference.

It was a kind and gentle school librarian, who can relate very little with the type of life I was suffering through, who came into the jail and led me to Christ. The Word of God and the Holy Spirit alone are anointed and powerful to convict and change a person's heart. A loving, kind witness can also partner with God to make known salvation which is available in Christ.

147

To date the Gideons alone have sent me to over 28 states, over half of the United States to share what God has done in my life. Specifically, my salvation experience in jail through the placing of the Word of God in my cell through a faithful Gideon Auxiliary member witnessing to me while incarcerated. It has been an honor and it continues to be an exciting journey of obedience.

Another incredible venue to share came in 2003 when Billy Graham came to Oklahoma. His foundation held an event at the Ford Center called "Mission Oklahoma City".

Oklahoma City Mayor Kirk Humphrey's, Baptist General Convention Executive Director Anthony Jordan, Charlie Daniel, Cliff Barrows, George Beverly Shea, Tait from DC Talk, and Kirk Franklin were some of the ones standing on the platform and performing.

It was brought to my attention by Don Duncan, who at the time was Director for Prison Fellowship in Oklahoma, when Billy Graham comes to a city, he also wanted to evangelize the prisons in the region.

Thus, the two-week evangelistic outreach events called, "Operation Starting Line" were planned. I was asked to attend the training day at the Baptist General Convention Building and prepare to share my testimony at a series of prison events over the two-week period.

This was an amazing time. They had invited some well-known and established music artists and presenters from all over the nation. How I made it into the mix is beyond me. I was so humbled and thankful to be amidst these people doing this good work. The event was set up to share what they called a "five-point gospel".

Each presenter was to share a point of the gospel while he or she also shared and flowed in the talent or gift the Holy Spirit had empowered them to share. Two of the points presented are God's Love and The Cross. Another of the five points I was assigned is, "Our Sin". Perfect! I had history and experience with sin and could cover those points well!

But, I could also relay the freedom I received from the slavery to sin. I was there for one reason - to bring glory to my Savior by telling the inmates Jesus is the only way out of sin, slavery, addiction, and darkness.

I shared my story many times in more than half of Oklahoma's prisons and several in Texas. The redemption and purpose I experienced, walking through the automatic steel gates of those prisons to testify of my Savior, is surreal and almost indescribable.

The response of the prisoners, men and women alike, I will never forget. So many approached the team and myself afterwards to surrender to Christ. Many shared exactly how they could relate to the speakers or asked for prayer for a specific area of their lives.

There is nothing which compares to being a clean vessel right where God wants you, doing what He has called you to do, and saying and expressing the truth He asks you to convey.

Being a part of a greater team with the same mission is also very rewarding. One day on the way to a men's prison, I was accompanied by a team of men and women and I was struggling a bit. I began to pray. "Lord, we are on our way to a men's prison. I am a woman. An open area full of men in prison will be looking and staring at me. What could I say which could offer men something to relate to or benefit from. I'll leave the part out about the abortions because men don't have abortions."

149

I continued to pour out my thoughts and concerns to the Lord in the van as we were on our way to the prison. The Lord simply responded, "I'm leading you. Share about the abortion, don't leave this part out". I didn't understand, but out of obedience I shared, as I had many times, about the abortions and forgiveness through Christ.

Immediately after the event a male prisoner came up to me with tears. "My wife had an abortion. I didn't want her to. I started drinking again when she did it and my drinking is what led me here to prison. When you shared about abortion it made me realize I needed to forgive her," he said.

I haven't argued with the Lord about sharing this part of my story again. I prayed with the man. There are many encounters like this which illustrate how God's power moved in the lives we ministered to, who received His Word as we traveled and shared.

I received a call one day from a young man. I answered the phone. He said, "Is this Barbara?" I said, "Yes, this is". He went on to share. "I got your written testimony through the sewer system while I was in prison. All the toilets were somehow connected, and another inmate pushed your testimony through to me. I read it and I want you to know it changed my life. It really spoke to me. I surrendered my life to Christ. I'm now out of prison and attending church at Henderson Hills. I'm preparing to go on a mission trip".

Praise God, what an encouragement! Through what one might describe as the sewage from a life of sin can come life-changing hope of a Savior.

Once I had shared my testimony and the Word of God in many different situations and circumstances for about 5 years including prisons, jails, youth detention centers, drug rehabs, conferences, retreats, seminars, schools, etc., I realized a desperate need for those who are incarcerated. There are many ministries and volunteer service programs available to inmates while in prison.

Free At Last Ministry presenting testimony at Laverne Highschool at "Meth Darkness" event. Lorene Witt, FAL administrative assistant. Christine England FAL recipient. Myself.

However, as I was sharing in these institutions and facilities throughout my state, I received a vision from the Lord for what is referred to as aftercare or prisoner re-entry ministry.

I sensed God leading to begin a ministry which would provide housing and discipleship to former prisoners particularly, but also to those in needy desperate situations who would reach out to us along the way.

Simply put, it was not enough to only go into the prison, jails and institutions sharing about salvation and freedom found in Christ only to turn around, leave, never to be seen again.

In 2005, Free At Last Ministries: A Ministry to Set the Captives Free was birthed. Free At Last Ministries, Inc. was established to help women re-enter society successfully after being incarcerated. It served as a 90-day Christ-centered ministry.

We provided; Housing and assistance, help in finding employment, transportation, weekly discipleship sessions, church attendance, daily bible study and prayer time, and Celebrate Recovery.

Monica, a Free At Last Ministry graduate receiving a standing ovation Sunday Morning Worship service after I presented her completion announcement and certificate.

It was our desire to provide a Christian "family" who would unconditionally love and support those who had prayerfully considered seriously changing their life.

God did some pretty special stuff and there were some mind-blowing connections made during the three-year ministry. Each person we had the opportunity to minister with is forever etched in my mind and heart.

Free At Last day of baptism's (Amy and Darcy)

I'll never forget the first lady who expressed a desire to come. Her name is Tabitha. I was sharing my testimony at the county jail in Claremore, Oklahoma while also in town speaking at a larger women's event taking place at the Baptist Church. While sharing,

I told the female inmates I had opened my home for discipleship after jail or prison. Tabitha didn't waste any time expressing interest. After she was released from jail she came to my home.

She stayed the 90-day limit, got a job and eventually worked at the church in housekeeping. We found her a little home to live after she graduated our ministry and she was reunited with her children.

Tabitha, our first special lady who came to Free At Last home. She's receiving "completion certificate"

Another lady who submitted application to come was Christine. Christine's application arrived, was reviewed, and accepted by the board. After her prison sentence was complete I drove to Taft, Oklahoma to pick her up the day she was released and walked out of Eddie Warrior Correctional Center.

Celebrate Recovery night included in Free At Last Ministry Christine, Amy, Lorene, myself.

During her stay with us, one Sunday morning she and my family were driving to church. On the way she was sharing openly about how she had lived with a family in Chickasha, Oklahoma during one of her high school years. I asked her, "What was the name of the family?" She stated, "The Fritz'. Norman Fritz."

I could hardly believe it!

Norman Fritz is the name of my biological brother, Robert's adopted Dad! I responded almost in disbelief and explained to Christine, Robert, "Bobby" had been adopted by the Fritz' and raised in Chickasha, Oklahoma. She said, "Yes, he would be the family." She went on to say she had been best friends with Robert's adopted sister, Tereasa.

Who is our God who orchestrates such intricate connections? I was mind-blown, again.

The ministry operated with a board of directors who represented five different denominations. The board met regularly to discuss and vote on the applications received from inmates inquiring to come. We also discussed progress of the ministry. The board helped in making decisions. First Baptist Church in Woodward, Oklahoma helped provide finances, as much as $1,000 per lady, per 90-day stay.

It was a very generous blessing for these ladies who, when released from jail or prison and who were likely in a true crisis, there isn't very much they don't need in terms of daily living and necessity items. "Palm Tree" Sunday school class provided necessity baskets for each person who came. "Dress For Success" ministry also made available clothing items for our people. We received donations including Life Recovery Bibles, clothing, and much more along the way from outside sources.

Lorene Witt served as an assistant and ministry partner. The hours she put in with transportation, meetings, and child care as I traveled to speak, as well as offering her administrative and organizational skills, were invaluable to the ministry. Most of all her faithful friendship and mother-like conversation, prayers, and sacrifices over the years are recognized and appreciated.

She wrote of the ministry,

"When Barbara and I started the Free At Last Ministry in 2005, we would get several women out of jail or prison to bring them to our small town of Mooreland, Oklahoma. They had no transportation, so we would help them get a job, board and room, take them to church, have Bible study and disciple them. Some of those women have been successful in their recovery and still keep in touch with Barbara."

Pastor Tony Barros spent hours in discipleship, counseling, behind the scenes administrative support, and words of knowledge and impartation of truth and direction freely given for those God led our way.

In 2001-2004 I was offered a unique opportunity to be a part of a new music company beginning in Nashville, Tennessee. The Christian Country Music Convention was held the first week of November. I was invited to speak at the hotel during the convention, help facilitate the prayer room, and present an award on the CCMA show, later named ICM (Inspirational Country Music) aired live on GAC (Great American Country) at the Ryman Auditorium otherwise known as the "Grand 'Ol Opry". This event was the culmination at end of the week. It was an exciting time.

Speaking, hosting prayer room, and presenting award live show aired on GAC at the Ryman in Nashville.

I enjoyed sharing my story at the convention and seeing it printed in Power Source Music Magazine. It was cool to see, meet, and appear on the same live show as some well-known singer and song writers such as Josh Turner, Jason Crabb, Crystal Gale, Hank Williams Jr., Fox Brothers, Jimmy Wayne, Jamie O'Neal and many others.

Some of the Christian songs on the charts up for awards during those years were "Long Black Train", "Jesus Take the Wheel", "Three Wooden Crosses", "I Love You This Much", and "Red, White, & Blue" to name a few.

There was a prayer room made available at the convention. The year I assisted in the prayer room I was partnered with Stella Parton, Dolly Parton's sister! It was a bit surreal as the resemblance was obvious. She shared with us and anyone who would listen about her upbringing in the Appalachian Mountains and her faith in Jesus. Mostly, I remember she called all believer's in Jesus, "God's babies".

These were powerful times of prayer. People from all over the United States attended and desired to network with other Christian Country Music artist and Professionals in the industry. I learned a lot.

I was humbled.

We also had the opportunity to hold sermon teaching sessions each day during the week. "Complete Deliverance", "Integrity In The Ministry", were two of the subjects we covered as well as my personal testimony story.

I was also prayed for and prophesied over. These were powerful words which came to pass and was consistent with who I am in Christ and the spiritual gifts and calling God had given.

Each year they also offered a contest. The winner would get to record a free 10-song project in the studio. I wanted to share this opportunity with a couple friends back home in Oklahoma at my church who I believed were excellent singers and song-writers.

One year I took Roma and another year I took Misty. Roma had an original song she sang and recorded while there called "Power in the Lamb". It made it to the top 100 in Christian Country List! Later, she recorded her first album titled, "The Dinner".

Misty came out another year to record her first couple songs. She wrote and recorded "The Blessing" and "Body of Christ". Both beautiful songs. Misty and I performed "Body of Christ" together. She sang, and I expressed the words in an exaggerated form of sign language. It was memorable. I was thankful to have friends to share opportunities God had graciously given.

I share my faith with those I come in contact with. I share about Jesus with people I run into at Wal-Mart, the grocery store, bank, and at the gym. Everywhere I go I hand out a small booklet of my testimony to people when the Holy Spirit nudges me to offer. I've passed out literally thousands of those pamphlets over the years.

By the grace of God, I have been able to pray with people from all walks of life. Holy Spirit would say to me while driving down the road as I saw a person walking, "Go pick up the person and talk about what I've done in your life with them". Or, "Pray with them", or share a particular scripture with them, "buy their meal, buy them or give them clothes or invite them to church or bible study."

I'll never forget a quadriplegic man I would see riding a special bike around town. His name is Ricky. The Lord asked me to stop and pray for this man. I kept running into him and asked him to come to church. Through God's people, we were able to provide a new living condition in a double-wide, health assistance, and transportation to and from our church services.

An unforgettable image in my mind is this man, so ready and willing to be baptized, he literally crawled on his elbows up three flights of stairs in our church to the baptistery to be baptized.

Ricky, the man who is quadriplegic who crawled up three flights of stairs to be baptized.

I will always remember a precious lady named Alicia. I was going in the same jail in Woodward county. Only now I went in willingly on the other side of the cell doors when Alicia responded at the bean hole one day. I shared some of my salvation story which took place right there in the very jail and prayed for her.

It was later when I was visiting homes during a visitation evening hosted by our church. I drove to the address listed on my card and walked up to the trailer.

Alicia answered the door! The same lady who I'd met in the jail.

She reluctantly showed me her wounded arm. There was a severe, at least 2nd to 3rd degree, large sized burn on it. She humbly confessed she had been cooking dope on the stove when it had blown up and the chemicals had landed on her arm.

I was truly concerned and offered to take her to the hospital. She declined and said she would treat it herself. She did accept some groceries I bought and offered her. She also let me visit and pray for her. I'm so thankful at the writing of the manuscript, Alicia has totally surrendered her life to Jesus and has been delivered from addiction. She is an active member of her church and is currently raising her granddaughter. Her countenance is completely transformed. I see Gods' light in and through her today.

These are Alicia's words after asking her if I could add some of her story to this chapter of the book:

"You were part of the heart, hands and feet of Jesus. I was one of the least of these, and you came. Then I saw you again in front of the store and God blessed me with you again, and again, and I'm still blessed by you and yours today. It's God's plan for His perfect story. We know and believe Jesus. He is good and will bring His fulfillment in our lives in Him to fruition."

Alicia made reference to this verse in a recent conversation:

Matthew 7:7-8 TPT Ask, and the gift is yours. Seek, and you'll discover. Knock, and the door will be opened for you. For every persistent one will get what he asks for. Every persistent seeker will discover what he longs for. And everyone who knocks persistently will one day find and open door."

159

Amen. I'm so proud of her and thankful Jesus saves, sets free, and restores! It is a beautiful and exciting thing to watch and be a part of.

DIVORCE

In the midst of full time ministry, several speaking engagements a month (a few occasions over the years where the girl's father and I both shared our testimonies at the same event), and raising my three school-age daughters, other problems continued to plague our lives.

About every few years evidence of infidelities or illegal activities on the part of their father would be brought to my attention by his hired hands. I would find pornography videos and cell phone records revealing the many women he was in contact with inappropriately. When confronted with the infidelities he would cry and get on his knees and beg for me to forgive him.

Painfully, I would.

I am a forgiven, set-free sinner myself and I wanted to extend mercy and grace to him as it had been extended to me. I also wanted a mom and dad together for my girls. He agreed to attend counseling a few times with me after one of the instances came to light. He would stay home a little longer and a bit more frequently after such truths came out.

However, it was short lived.

He had a construction business requiring him to be gone most the time, as was his custom. I would wonder where he was and what he was doing. Why was he gone so much of the time? I would ask him but get no answers, or only lies. On occasion, he would make it home late on a Saturday night, get up and attend church with the girls and me, and whoever may be staying at the ministry dorm.

Around this same time, a man who worked for him knocked on my back door. He was a man who had been well acquainted with him for many years off and on. He had begun working for him again because he had surrendered his life to Jesus and my husband had told him he had a "Christian business".

With tears streaming down his face, he poured out his concern mixed with great fear. He pleaded with me to understand my husband was not living a Christian life. He was not running a Christian business. It was anything but truth. He said there was such a depth of evil going on he was scared and leaving for good. He just wanted me to know before he left.

The sincere pain and intense panic in this former biker and previous drug dealer's eyes gripped me with fear, and in turn caused my heart to sink once again.

During my daughters 12th birthday at our home, an FBI agent, who also happened to be a deacon in my church, rang the doorbell. When I answered the door, the agent asked for him by name. He went out to his car and stayed there talking for quite some time. He came back in, grabbed some items and left with the agent. While he was gone, I packed up all his clothes and personal items and took them to his office, a separate building from the house. This scene taking place during our daughter's birthday party was heartbreaking and caused great anger within me.

His story, the next time I spoke with him, was he helped the agents bust the guy who robbed some banks in Oklahoma City. He went on to say he wore a wire while having dinner with a man who worked for him, who confessed to using his company van and robbing the banks while in possession of his vehicle.

He was awarded a hundred-dollar check later for helping solve a bank robbery. At this point, I didn't believe a word he said. There were just too many "coincidences" like this over the years.

Police, retired sheriffs, FBI, and later OBN (Oklahoma Bureau of Narcotics) and OSBI (Oklahoma Bureau of Investigation), would give me information about ongoing illegal involvements of all sorts he was either directly involved in or involved in an ancillary way. Not long after the supposed bank robbery investigation, the same Federal agent (FBI) approached me at church. He asked if he could talk to me.

We stepped away from the crowd and he began asking me questions like, "What are you doing with this guy? Do you love him?" I was confused.

I said, "What do you mean? He is the father of my children. Yes, I have a love for him," I said. "I am a Christian. I am a believer. I'm to be faithful and not separate or divorce my husband." He started by saying, "I'm going to tell you some things, but because of my position if anyone ever asked me about it I would deny it."

He continued by saying, "I've been watching this situation for years with an on-going investigation. It's just not right. Here you are, you have changed your life and here he is living a double life. These guys come to church and put on a front. They claim they are a Christian and still live a crooked life."

163

He continued, "I catch bad guys. There are bad guys. Then there are really bad guys. Your husband is a really bad guy." He finally told me he knew he was dealing dope, committing embezzlement, money laundering and owned land with stolen property on it.

He even mentioned an exact room number at a hotel in Texas, where he was dealing drugs and where prostitutes would come and go on a regular basis. I was still confused. Why would they have an investigation and all this awareness of illegal activity, but do nothing to bring him to accountability and justice? Why didn't they just arrest him?

Reality or not, due to the recent bank robbery scenario and stories over the years, what I perceived was the law using him to turn in others, to help them arrest others.

A deacon and Sunday school teacher in my church who I knew was respected, who loved his entire family, stood before me. At the same time, this same man, a federal agent spoke these things with a sincere yet serious look.

I realized God had prompted him to take the risk to disclose these specifics.

On the other hand, I thought, what good is this? I have been told these things, but what am I supposed to do with information which would be denied if I attempted to do anything about it? It was as if my heart fell out of my chest onto the floor while he was talking. I had such a sinking feeling.

Tremendous pain and sadness mixed with weariness and fear came over me.

I had been praying over very specific questions I had for God. God, where is my husband? What is he doing? Why doesn't he call? Why doesn't he come home much? Why doesn't he want to spend time with me and his children? The answer had come.

I wanted to believe he had changed. I wanted to believe he was the man he said he had become. I wanted my girls to have their mom and dad together and a dad who was present and available. I was sharing publicly in my testimony how God reconciled our marriage. He had even shared his testimony with me on occasion where God was the greatest "high" there is, and God had provided him with a million dollar a year Christian company.

However, time had now revealed the truth.

Here I was again, presented with the character and actions of a man who consistently deceived me. God answered my questions specifically. I could not keep hiding my head in the sand and pretend he hadn't. I had a choice to make.

After much prayer and Godly counsel, I filed for divorce.

Despite tremendous fear and anxiety about what he might do to me or have someone else do to me, I decided to take the risk to value myself and believe what God said about me and my girls.

Marriage was to be mutual love and respect. Years and years of ongoing lies, unrepentant adultery, criminal involvement, and deception is not God's idea of covenant marriage. I realized there was no easy decision. My daughters would hurt either way. I settled on an answer. I would take the risk of fully grieving the loss of hope for a healthy marriage with their father.

I surrendered.

I also did all I knew to do to help my girls walk through the process of healing. We all spent time with Christian counselors/pastors through this very difficult time and transition.

When this divorce was final, the girls and I stayed in the home we lived in and I kept my car. I had primary custody of my three daughters. He had standard visitation every other weekend.

At this point, I was finally able to prove his ability to pay sufficient child support based on what he had already been paying monthly upon the Child Support Division's determination. He remained owner of the business, equipment, and his vehicles.

REDEMPTION

*So, if the Son sets you free, you will be free
indeed. (TPT) John 8:36*

Because of divorce, the re-entry housing portion of Free At Last Ministries had to stop. I needed to begin working full time. I began working for an optometrist. After approximately six months the physician became too ill and needed to downsize.

My pastor then told me of a small company opportunity. I took the online tests, received my personal stamp and became a Notary Signing Agent. I named my company Lighthouse Notary & Signing Agent Services, Inc.

I would travel to different homes and act as an impartial third-party witness to the signing of loan documents and remortgages. This served as sufficient supplemental income during the difficult transition of divorce and discovering a new normal.

I determined I would use the opportunities of traveling and meeting couples and families in their homes to share my faith and testimony when God's Spirit nudged me. After business was completed I would offer my written testimony pamphlet.

Many divine appointments, heartfelt conversations, and sincere prayers were experienced during these business closings. A couple encounters stand out and remain with me.

I scheduled a remortgage at a couple's home in a small town near Enid, Oklahoma one day. When I arrived, we began the usual process of signing and notarizing the mortgage paperwork. I witnessed the two names of the signers being written over and over again in a packet of over a hundred papers.

While glancing around the house I noticed certificates from Meadowlake Hospital. It took a little time, but I began to recognize these two people. It suddenly occurred to me these two people were working at the juvenile institution on the same unit I lived on in Enid when I was thirteen and fourteen years old!

I mentioned, "I think I recognize you both" I said, "You probably do not remember me but the both of you worked on the unit at the institution I was in". They were surprised. She got up, went to another room, came back with a photo album. She began showing pictures from Meadowlake! It was indeed the same folks all these years later.

I had been participating in a bible study at my church during this time called, "Believing God". It was also by author and speaker, Beth Moore. She was a huge influence in my spiritual growth for the first ten years of my walk with God. Just prior to meeting back up with this couple, I was deep into the curriculum and daily assignments.

Week 7 was titled, "Believing God Has Been There All Along" subtitled: "A Different Kind of Memory Retrieval". On page 143 it stated,

"We're going to look back and see what treasures we can find, sometimes even in the midst of rubble. Like detectives searching for evidence, we'll look for the fingerprints our invisible God interspersed throughout our lives. Beloved, God has been there all along--even before we acknowledged Him as Savior. He is the infinite, eternal, omnipresent God who woos to His heart those who will draw near. It's time for some positive memory retrieval, Dear One. The kind that edifies rather than terrifies....

Over the next two weeks in the Faith Journal section you are going to write your own book of your personal journey with God. Whether or not you realize it, you have a book inside you! Let's get some of it down on paper. Please participate fully....I pray this journal will become priceless to you and your children."

This was such a huge confirmation as Father God had already asked me to write a book which would be a longer version of my story I had been sharing publicly. I took a risk and shared this with the bible study group the first night in response to the question posed to the group, "What are you believing God for?"

Under the heading, "Lord, the biggest challenges I have before me right now are…" I filled in the blank, **"Believing you for a book/movie"**

At this time, I began the suggested seven-year increment outline based on how old I was (34 years old). It was to be the outline I would use for answering the questions in the study as well as the outline for the book I would begin writing by faith.

And, begin writing I certainly did.

169

It was the journal for the first seven years of my life where my perspective began to be transformed from having been abandoned to having been RESCUED by God. I began the journal questions for my life, ages 7-14, when I had the divine encounter with the couple who worked at Meadowlake institution.

This visit was a powerful day. It was transformative.

My eyes were opened even more to the fact God was ordaining my steps, leading me into appointments which were not only confirmations I was hearing His voice clearly in the writing of the book, but also the healing which came in the process.

I left the couple's home having to stop at the end of the drive, weeping yet sensing the intricate redemption of God. I continued to worship my King all the way back home.

What a Master Architect! He was always busy crafting and building our lives. Once again, I was mind-blown.

Another encounter pertaining to healing and redemption occurred not long after this one. I was called to do a closing for another couple. Again, I copied the documents and drove to their home.

Toward the end of the closing, after the couple had signed their last name over and over I couldn't help but notice it was the same last name as the older of the two men who had purchased me at age 17 for the purpose of making me an escort, prostitute, and for sexual slavery.

I cautiously asked if they happened to be kin to him (I stated his name to them). The man said, "Yes, He was my brother". He then asked me how I knew his brother. I was reluctant.

However, he encouraged me saying he knew the kind of man his brother was, stating, "He couldn't change to save his life." Mustering up some courage, I handed him a copy of my testimony booklet, as was my habit to do at each closing.

I then briefly shared how I met his brother, as well as my salvation and how Jesus had changed my life up to this point. Then he and his wife shared with me they just so happened to be pastors and asked if I would come share my story at their church! Wait, What?! They were so loving, accepting, and understanding.

It was incredibly healing and freeing to be embraced by the family of the very man who enslaved me as a teenager. To be asked and allowed to come and share my testimony in their church is beyond words. It helped me let it go, forgive, and heal.

Who is this amazing God we serve who orchestrates such intimate, intricate details? I want to know Him! I want to serve Him! I was making some tremendous progress on the manuscript and experiencing great strides of healing in the process.

I continued to struggle, however, with fear. Specifically fear of men. The thought of dating terrified me. I really hadn't been able to mature in this area of my life.

I was given a name of a Christian counseling ministry in Oklahoma City named Grace Given Ministries by a pastor whom I trusted. These sessions consisted mostly of addressing fear I continued to wrestle with and recognizing and learning to identify the God-given healthy desire within me. I was gaining freedom over fear of death, dating, and men. Well, at least I was addressing and discussing these issues.

A few years after the divorce and after counseling a man began attending our single Sunday school class movie nights. He asked me to date him. I agreed I would try.

Not long after this my oldest daughter began to express a desire to date. She was fourteen-years-old. I had already set the age of sixteen as the age I would begin considering this. In my opinion she was too young.

As a result of the divorce and visiting schedule, she would spend time every other weekend with her dad and his family. Her behavior more and more began to be out of character for her; rudeness and rebelliousness.

Soon she began demanding to go live with her dad, so she could date and have more freedom to do as she wanted. As far as I was concerned this was not an option nor should it ever be.

After much biblical counseling, I began feeling some freedom and courage to begin a dating process. In my opinion this progress in me did not equate to my daughter being old enough or mature enough to do the same.

Her father continued to operate in the same business and manner revealed to me by the law and investigators. This environment was no place for a young teenage girl.

She continued to press and threaten me to say, "The law says when I turn fourteen I have a choice of where I want to live." And, "If you don't let me go live with my dad so I can date I'll tell the judge you abuse me." It appeared as if she had a source who was educating and coaching my daughter on a broader level of legal options and maneuvers.

My daughter's stark shift in behavior and the accusations hurled at me were shocking. I responded in anger and fear at times. I feared her father as well as his family's influence on her.

Up to this point, and to my relief and surprise, their dad basically left me alone until he discovered I was dating a man and attempting to move on with my life. However, now he began calling me and making cruel, indecent, untrue accusations including rolling down the window and yelling obscenities at me from his vehicle when dropping off the girls from his time of visitation.

He would threaten to kill me and the man I was dating when I would answer his phone calls. Then, late in the evenings there appeared to be bright head-lights shone directly in my French-style patio back doors for long periods of time. I was too scared to walk outside.

I would confess my fear in prayer.

I went to a farm and ranch store called Atwoods one day, which was out of the ordinary for me to do. I was looking through a barrel of bandanas when I saw one which stood out. In the whole mix of solid-colored bandanas, I spotted a camouflage one. When I held it up it had the entire Psalm 91 versed in black bold print on it! I could hardly believe it.

I looked again, rummaging through the barrel, then looking all around me. There were no other bandanas with bible verses on them.

I stood there in the middle of the store and read the entire Psalm out loud with tears of amazement:

PSALM 91

He who dwells in the secret place of the Most High

Shall abide under the shadow of the Almighty.

I will say of the Lord, He is my refuge and my fortress;

My God, in Him I will trust.

Surely, He shall deliver me from the snare of the fowler

And from the perilous pestilence.

He shall cover me with His feathers,

And under His wings I shall take refuge;

His truth shall be my shield and buckler.

I shall not be afraid of the terror by night,

Nor of the arrow that flies by day,

Nor of the pestilence that walks in darkness,

Nor of the destruction that lays waste at noonday.

A thousand may fall at my side,

And ten thousand at my right hand;

But it shall not come near me.

Only with my eyes shall I look and see the reward of the wicked.

*Because I have made the Lord, Who is my
refuge,*

Even the Most High, my dwelling place,

*No evil shall befall me, Nor shall any plague
come near my dwelling;*

*For He shall give His angels charge over me, To
keep me in all my ways.*

*In their hands they shall bear me up, Lest I dash
my foot against a stone.*

I shall tread upon the lion and the cobra,

*The young lion and the serpent I shall trample
underfoot.*

*Because I have set my love upon Him, therefore
He will deliver me;*

*He will set me on high because I have known His
name.*

I shall call upon Him, and He will answer me.

*He will be with me in trouble; He will deliver me
and honor me*

*He with long life will satisfy me and show me His
salvation.*

I memorized the first portion of the Psalm after rehearsing it so
many times. I hung the bandana on a pillar over my bed. So, as I was
falling asleep at night I would see the bandana, recite the verse, and it
would help me to not give way to fear knowing the Lord Himself was
watching over and protecting me and my girls.

175

Bandana of Psalm 91 I kept on the pillow of my bed reminding myself of God's protection to calm my fears when falling asleep at night.

He would show up at Wal-Mart and various places where the man I was dating would go. My date sensed he was being stalked and followed, in an attempt to intimidate and scare him away from me.

I didn't know the best way to handle this position. The old familiar fear of him surfaced, it never fully disappeared, only lay dormant when I wasn't faced with his threats or have to directly talk or deal with him. My survival response triggered.

I decided to apply for a protective order.

The man I was dating and I both went to the courthouse and filled out the application for an emergency protective order. We were both called into Judge's chambers and explained what was going on and why we were asking the court for the protective order.

On July 6, 2010 we were granted an emergency protective order including preventing their father's visitation with the girls temporarily. There was another hearing scheduled to present testimony.

I contacted a friend whose husband was an attorney. I retained him to represent me. He stuck with us and represented my girls and me through the entire grueling court processes for well over the next year.

Unfortunately, the protective order was dropped.

Their father also retained an attorney, who arranged for what they called a relocation hearing. It was an attempt to prevent me from moving.

In hope of subsiding the fear and anxiety I was experiencing prior to the hearing, I was reading and reciting over and over in my mind and out loud:

> *Luke 12:11-12 When you are brought before the synagogues, rulers and authorities, do not worry about how you will defend yourselves or what you will say, for the Holy Spirit will teach you at that time what you should say.*

Despite my plan to remain calm, confident, and collected, the sight of him and his presence in the courtroom intimidated me into a fear response. I shut-down and didn't know how to respond to the bombardment of probing questions by his attorney. It was humiliating.

This court hearing consisted of forceful question after question. I literally could not speak or find the words to defend or explain myself. I did manage to voice some explanation - the move was because I was soon to be married, and I was moving on the farm where my new husband lived.

I also described the move as being obedient to God's voice and direction in my life at this time. The judge's decision was to restrain my move. We did, however, marry on August 8, 2010.

Due to the high amount of stress, fear, and pain for almost the next two years, I will do my best to account for the general details. I have also done my best to recall the sequence of events, as I was operating in survival. I felt like I needed to fight for the safety of my girls. It was traumatic, at best.

Spiritually speaking, I entered what might be described as a long season of severe testing and pruning. No stone left unturned.

Father God never left.

I sensed when he wasn't carrying me, He was walking by my side and was faithful to protect and restore. Holy Spirit resides within me. I remained in the Word of God and worshipped my way through this deep, dry valley.

During the time when the judge had suspended visitation with their father, I calmly explained to my daughters they were not going to stay the weekend with him because of the emergency protective order by the judge.

My oldest was enraged. She began yelling obscenities similar to the comments her father had said to me before. I told her to go to her room. Later, in the middle of the night, my daughter woke me up crying saying, "I'm sorry Mom, I'm sorry Mom. I didn't mean it".

She confessed to taking some over the counter pills. I took her to the hospital, where they kept her overnight for observation and discharged her the next day. I agreed to resume some counseling for her with our youth pastor.

After returning home, things did not get better.

My daughter was increasingly defiant and insistent on living with her dad. She screamed and cussed at me and refused to do anything I asked of her. I was afraid for my other two daughters and myself. We were in the kitchen one afternoon when she raised her hand to hit me in the face. I reached out to block this and held her arms firmly, so as to keep them at her side. I explained she was not going to hit me and treat me this way.

After holding her arms out of self-defense for what seemed like a few minutes, she continued to yell and scream at me. I let go of her arms and told her to go to her room. One day she didn't come home. I called the police to report. The police found her at her father's sister's house. They brought her back home.

Another day she started in on her threats and vulgarities, I told her to go lean over her bed. I came in with a belt and spanked her. I rarely felt the need to use spanking as a type of discipline or correction. I could count on both hands how many times I spanked all three of my kids.

Due to the behavior she was manifesting however, spanking was a desperate attempt at getting her attention and letting her know her actions were not appropriate, nor was I going to tolerate the disrespect and physical confrontation.

She left the house. The police brought her back home again but this time I was given the option and decided to have her stay at the youth shelter for the night to keep her safe due to her running away. While at the youth shelter she wrote out reports I had allegedly abused her.

They took her to a pediatrician in town who utilized what they called a "Woodson stick" which was described to me as an ultraviolet light to reveal markings on her buttocks where I had spanked her. This was categorized by them as 'abuse' due to the invisible mark they discovered.

An emergency custody hearing was filed by their father and family where they had my daughters testify. They also had a representative from DHS get involved and gave their opinions, as well, without ever speaking to or interviewing me first.

At the time of the emergency custody hearing there were multiple people present at the courthouse from my church ready and willing to testify on my behalf and in the best interest of my girls.

We were all in a little room praying and waiting for our chance to present our case. We never got a chance. What seemed like an eternity later, my attorney came in told me the judge awarded their father emergency temporary custody and another court date was set to follow-up on the case and decide permanence.

My children were told they did not have to visit me, only if they wanted to. And, it would need to be supervised visitation for short intervals. Once again, it is very difficult to find words to describe the shock and devastation in my heart. I remember a general physical weakness coming over me and could barely stand.

Nevertheless, I stood watching my girls on the other side of the hall in the courthouse, having just learned of the judge's decision to place all three of my children in the temporary custody of their father. Only Father God truly knows what struck my heart in those moments.

It is beyond my capability of understanding how I made it through the extreme addiction and incarcerations without permanently losing or being manipulated to relinquish custody of my girls.

Yet, there I stood. Eleven years of sobriety and salvation, devoting myself to Christ, His service, His word, raising my girls in purity and truth and still they were taken away from me.

Luke 22:42 -"Father, if you are willing, take this cup from me; yet not my will, but yours be done."

My greatest fear became a reality in those oppressive moments. The very thing I worked so hard to prevent from happening, cooperating with and allowing the Holy Spirit to invade and change my life, identity, and direction, to live sober, sane, and be a safe mother to my girls, felt shattered on this day.

What appeared to be a game of power and control to the ones manipulating my vulnerable children, certainly was not a win or lose verdict to me. What happened the months prior to and solidified the day through a human judge was the work of an enemy.

Jesus speaking: John 10:10 A thief has only one thing in mind-he wants to steal, slaughter, and destroy. But I have come to give you everything in abundance, more than you expect—life in its fullness until you overflow! TPT

This attack did not come from hearts of love and true concern for the safety, well-being, and health of my children, as evidenced by the scary and serious situations they were all three subjected to soon after their move.

After a long and brutal wait, my husband at the time and I, made our way out of the courthouse to my vehicle. I drove to a restaurant parking lot and stopped the car.

I sat there in the driver's seat. I was shocked and horrified by the scene which just took place at the courthouse. A cross I had hanging on the rear-view mirror came into view and focus. The pain seized me.

I reached up, grabbed the cross and tore it down from the mirror. For those next initial moments, I expressed my anger and confusion to God. I assure you my expressions were not pretty, polite, or properly postured.

My most precious possessions had been manipulated and now were victims of a deception and a system which let them and me down. A lady from the Department of Human Services testified to the judge at my hearing. The same afternoon, I went to the DHS office just down the road. I sat down and spoke with her about what just happened in court.

I had more than a few questions and statements regarding how my three children could be taken from a safe Christian home and put with a man who was mostly on the road, and a known drug dealer among law enforcement, as well as other serious allegations. She stated the calls to their office were about me as the abuser; not an investigation about their father. She suggested I attend parenting and anger management classes.

I took her suggestion and drove the two hours round trip for eighteen weeks of parenting classes and twelve weeks of anger management classes held at the Assembly of God in Woodward, Oklahoma.

In fact, I submitted to all they suggested and relied on the Spirit of God within me to remain teachable and humble. If my behavior and decisions in response to this judicial atrocity would determine the future possibility of my girls being rescued and returned to my home, then I wanted to do my best despite my pain, anger, and questions, and allow God to be my Defender and my children's Deliverer.

I wept off and on during the day and cried myself to sleep every night for months.

I began jogging with our Great Dane to try and run off some of the pain, sorrow, and anger. I lived in a farm house on a hill in the middle of wheat and crops. As far as I could see in any direction was fields. I worked up to running the section square. I'd get to the end of one-mile corner, be overtaken by grief and anger, stop and scream at the top of my lungs,

"WHY GOD? WHY?"

I spent most my time in the Psalms and developed an appreciation and understanding for the life of Job. I stenciled and painted Job 19:25 on the huge propane tank outside the window near the farmhouse where I was living. I painted it there as a reminder and a bold, black lettered statement of faith in the midst of fear and despair:

JOB 19:25 I KNOW MY REDEEMER LIVES

The entire verse reads, "I know my redeemer lives, and that in the end he will stand on the earth."

Another one from the book of Job I found hopeful was

JOB 23:10 But He knows the way that I take;
when he has tested me, I will come forth as gold.

I had to arrive at a place mentally and emotionally, in which I offered my most precious possessions, my daughters to God. Similarly, to Abraham placing Isaac on the altar of sacrifice in the old testament, I surrendered them to Father's hands under His watch, care, and protection.

Otherwise, this would have killed me.

I was extremely afraid for my girls. It wasn't only my former family had sided, supported, and influenced my daughters to accuse and become a witness against me in a court with serious allegations of abuse. But I was sincerely and deeply concerned for their health, purity, and safety. Let us not forget who this man was in my own life for years and where he learned to know me.

Since my salvation and transformation in 1998, I vowed to raise my girls in a sober home and in the Lord. I took this commitment seriously.

During the year and two months they lived with their father, proof and confessions revealed they were exposed to drugs, alcohol, people who did drugs and dealt them, as well as myriad immoral and illegal behaviors. What I had been powerfully and graciously delivered from, they had now been sucked into.

One of my greatest fears was being played out.

I stayed with and succumbed to their father's control over the years for different reasons. One of the most overwhelming reasons was I was terrified he or his family would get custody of my children and lead them into their lifestyle and influence them into their deceptive way of life.

All this legal process and judicial involvement was very difficult for my husband (at this time) to witness. I had finally remarried and had felt this was a new beginning for me. Now, he too was devastated by what was playing out. He lost all confidence in the courts, law enforcement officers and our judicial system in general.

Ironically, during this same time a friend introduced me to a State Representative Blackwell who was actively involved with what was described to us as an "interim study on DHS" in Oklahoma at the capital. Some of their practices and policies were being investigated and questioned. We connected with him, sharing the immediate situation we were in involving DHS, having testified in the hearing contributing to and resulting in the removal of all three of my minor children being placed in an unsafe, detrimental environment.

He invited us to come share testimony of our situation at the hearing taking place at the state capital in Oklahoma City. At these proceedings I was able to speak and testify of my side, something I was not given the chance to do at the Woodward courthouse the day the ruling was rendered to remove my children.

I stood before the State Supreme Court including a large room of people and shared the factual details during the process of how my children were taken from my home and placed with their father, including DHS' role and involvement in the process. The general response was even though DHS was called and became involved in testifying at the emergency custody hearing, it was ultimately the district judge, Don Work's final decision to remove my children and place them with their father. Somehow it diminished and dissolved DHS' responsibility in their opinion.

My girls had very little supervision, structure, or discipline now. My middle daughter took on a new identity and wanted to be known by a new name "D-Money or D$". She was caught with and began selling prescription medications and pot at school. Her grades dropped severely. She also started a fire.

At one point a girl died from what was said or suspected to be an overdose. The OSBI continued to call and ask my daughter to testify regarding events she may have witnessed at her father's home in relation to a man raping this girl, after she had already passed away. I sat with my daughter in their office while they asked her questions related to this event much later.

I felt anger.

My heart broke for my daughter and the girl's family who died. It was a family whom I spoke with later. I maintained visitation with my youngest daughter only. My oldest daughter did not come visit. My middle daughter called and visited a couple times in a little over a year. They maintained they were old enough to decide whether they wanted to honor the visitation or not.

I was in the process of selling my home now, married and having moved to where he and his family were located. This meant a new home, farm culture, and a new church

After marrying and moving, while it was on the market, my home got broken into. There was furniture and personal items including photo albums of my girls stolen. There was other evidence of someone, multiple persons, being there.

The intruders left a window open. Being winter it got so cold one night my home flooded due to a pipe bursting. I was sharing my testimony in another state and on my way home, when I decided to stop by and check on my home for sale.

Thank goodness I did! As I walked up the front porch steps I could hear rushing water.

I'm not sure how long the water had been gushing out. But the damage was extensive. I had to reduce the asking price significantly to sell. I eventually sold my home on April 4, 2011, eight months after I had married and moved to the farm.

I was then able to purchase another home 7 miles south of the ranch where I was living with my husband at the time. This was only about an hour away from where my girls remained.

The final custody hearing kept being postponed for one reason or another. One time it was postponed because their father's attorney was arrested for attempting to help her boyfriend escape from a prison. She also was actively engaging in illegal drug use. With her new charges pending, it suspended her legal right to practice law and in turn she retired from the case.

As difficult as the waiting was, God was at work arranging what only He alone could do to bring my children back to our home and a safe place.

During this excruciating battle, we waited, waited some more and all the while continued to walk with the Lord while my children were not living with me. I couldn't help but become aware of some ironies and glaring similarities in the sharp change of attitude and behavior I went through as a new teenage girl in light of what my oldest daughter's behavior was turning into.

Only now, I was on the other side of the table. I was the mom having to decide and make the hard decisions of how I was going to react and respond. I began to experience understanding and compassion for my mom and what she could have possibly been feeling when I was a teenager making the decisions I was.

During this time, I was listening to a Christian radio station. I liked a program called, "Family Life Today". They were interviewing Dennis and Barbara Rainey about the book they wrote called, "How To Write A Tribute To Your Parents" based on the verse *Exodus 20:12,* which comes from the Ten Commandments:

"Honor your father and your mother, that your days may be long in the land that the Lord your God is giving you"

I ordered and read this book. I was moved by the message. This realization was so intense considering the immediate dynamic with my daughters and how it paralleled with what my mom and I went through beginning with my teenage years. It led me to write a tribute to my mom.

I knew God was speaking to me and wanted to utilize all which was happening with my girls for good and for healing. It took my daughters' decisions to open my eyes to my mom's perspective. My mom and I had taken many steps toward forgiveness over the years. But after hearing the radio interview and reading this book, I knew I needed to take this next step and write a tribute.

The writers of the book advised there weren't any specific rules. It only needed to be from the heart and to be willing to look at your parents through the eyes of Christ. Not only did I write the tribute, I wanted it to be a formal and special evening. So, I invited her out to dinner at one of her favorite restaurants and presented it to her right at the table.

With tears I honored my mom. This was the poem I wrote and framed.

LAVONNE ELAINE SHOOPMAN SAUNDERS KISER

God chose you to be my mom
Your temporary inability?
NO
Father's Sovereignty!
Rescued to refuge
Safety, sanity, security....calm and clean
MOM and DAD
LaVonne and Dean

You worked so hard
Day after day
Willingly and wantingly
Granting us opportunity to play

I'll never forget
That special race
When in a fall....the dog poop
You did embrace :-)

Fun times we had
Good memories were made
Holidays, seasons, trips to the lake
Birthday parties, blue birds, riding my bike to meet friends
down Glade.
A standard of excellence
Integrity you showed
An example of dedication
Image of devotion to husband and family I'll hold

Then the time came
Who knew?
The storm coming;
Hail pounded, and the rains blew

Very little the torrents didn't hit
So much was taken
Rebellion, addiction, death, and desperation
We were all cruelly awakened

Your response....
With all the strength you had
Determination to go to college
Anticipating life without husband or dad

Long days of classes and homework
Endless nights studying
In a couple short moments
GRADUATING!!!

Doing what you love
In the classroom all those years
Teaching the children
And I'm sure sowing in a few tears

You respected and honored your parents
Although with everything you didn't agree
It remains
A solid example for me

Raising my children now
It's true what they say
Until you're a parent yourself
One cannot understand the way

About our own families and lives
Graceful and redeeming words we saw you write
You're proud of us all

Each of us, individually, in your sight

I knew victory had arrived
When I heard you speak
Please go and read Hosea 6:1
It had summed it up for you that week

When I opened my Bible tears of joy came
It was true
Evidence from His Word
God was leading us out and through!

Growing closer now
Learning to be forgiven and forgive
Mom, this is a tribute to you
For helping me to live.

Your Daughter,
Barbara

Come on, let's go back to GOD.
He hurt us, but He'll heal us.
He hit us hard, but He'll put us right again.
Hosea 6:1
"Honor your father and mother...." Exodus 20:12

I purchased a four-bedroom home in faith, believing with no obvious evidence at the time God would return my children.

I began remodeling the house. I worked on it the entire year my girls were in their father's custody. I would turn on worship music, mostly Selah, and through my heart-wrenching grief and tears I would work, tearing out cabinets, stripping and re-staining doors, scraping wallpaper, texturing and painting everything outside and inside. New kitchen tops, floors and light fixtures were installed. As I labored, it was a release of anger and fear of what my children and I were going through.

On November 28, 2011, we finally received custody of my youngest daughter first without having a court hearing. Her dad agreed. She needed more supervision than he could provide, and he confessed she also needed her mom. She came to live with us and we got her into our nearest public school.

I was so very thankful. God was at work.

My youngest daughter told me where the belongings were located which had been stolen from my house including TV's, VCR's, Picture albums, bedroom furniture, television/DVD stand. She described exactly on her father's property where they were located and made a written statement. The police went there and were able to retrieve most of the stolen property. January 13, 2012 an order from the judge was signed to return all stolen property to me. The photo albums of my girls were the most important to me to have returned.

One of the favorites of my three babies

Not long after this, I received a phone call one day from Jan, my oldest daughters' former youth group church leader. She had been allowing my middle daughter to stay there for a short time because her dad stated he could no longer "control" her. She informed me their dad had been arrested. She didn't know the details. She thought it was possession and distribution of drugs. She also stated she thought the law had raided where he lived.

After our conversation, I hung up the phone and immediately hit my knees in worship. I began thanking God He was making a way. I thanked Him He was bringing truth into light. I continued to cry and worship.

With their father in jail now, I could get my girls back home! It had been a very long, excruciating year and two months. On Thursday, January 12, 2012, on the front page of The Mooreland Leader an article stated more details of his arrest:

"A 61-year-old Mooreland man was arrested and taken to the Woodward County Jail after a search warrant was served at his residence (address) early Thursday morning, Jan 5. The search warrant was served by agents of Oklahoma Bureau of Narcotics and Dangerous Drugs."

Went on to say he was arrested for: "maintaining a dwelling where controlled dangerous substance (CDS) is kept, conspiracy to distribute/deliver CDS, and endeavoring to unlawfully possess a controlled dangerous substance (prescription pills)."

"The search resulted in seizure of multiple prescription pill bottles with labels other than (his name), multiple used syringes and several metal spoons that contained a burned crystal-like substance. Oklahoma Bureau of Narcotics and Dangerous Drugs Woodward District Officer in Charge Wendell Brandenburg said, "We are still investigating a number of people from Watonga and Sayre that are tied to the illegal sale and trade of legal prescription drugs. We anticipate more arrests in the near future."

"Aiding in the service of the search warrant were Mooreland Police Department, Woodward County Sherriff's office, Oklahoma Bureau of Investigation and Federal Bureau of Investigation."

On January 19, 2012 I went to the courthouse and stood before the judge who had ruled to remove my children from my home and place them with their father. The deputy brought up their father from the basement jail cell in an orange suit. The judge pronounced due to their father's newly current arrest, charges and pending sentencing; emergency full custody of my children was placed back with me.

God won the victory!

I wouldn't wish incarceration on anyone. However, just like God had accomplished through my jail time, I was thankful for the multiple purposes seemingly being met with their father's arrest. I offer no explanation for the return of my children being nothing other than divine intervention.

Back to court on a later date for the final custody hearing the judge announced the decision. The girls were placed back in my permanent custody. The rebuttal and angry protest from my oldest daughter began right there in the courtroom. The screaming got so loud the court officials had to shut it down.

We finally got them in the car. The hour ride from the courthouse to the farm house consisted of my oldest two daughters screaming at the top of their lungs.

The environment they had been in allowed them to do and be "free" to do basically whatever they wanted. This proved to be entirely detrimental. Turns out they basically lived in a place where drugs were being used and distributed for over a year now despite my pleas to the judge, DHS, and anyone else who would listen.

My daughters responded in a manner in which I had been taught was disrespectful and destructive. The "abuse" they accused me of is how they themselves reacted and behaved. They yelled, hit, destroyed property, refused to do anything expected or asked of them. I did not recognize my oldest girls.

They soon set up a "plan" to run away. They found a way to communicate with one of their father's family members and asked her to pick them up at one of the nearest gas stations once they had run away. Their plan was in motion until the police noticed them at the gas station and I was called. This person was later told by legal officials to stop interfering.

The next months were chaos. The days consisted of constant rebellious behavior and the stress of not knowing what they would do next. Being cussed at, physically attacked by my daughters, destruction of property, running away, and possessing marijuana, all contributed to my oldest two being put into a youth detention center.

DHS involvement and previous allegations made about me abusing my children, the main event being spanking my oldest daughter over a year prior and leaving a mark on her buttocks, is one of the ways which got my children placed with their father.

It stole my ability to now discipline them in any sort of physical method. When they attacked me physically, holding me down, punching me, hitting me, kicking me I would hunch down on the ground trying to cover my head and face with my hands. I didn't fight back or defend myself.

All I had left when they behaved with running away, violence, and illegal activity was to call the police. I lost count how many times Beaver county officers came out to the farm house. To correct and gain authority over the situation, the officer would hand-cuff the girls and place them in the back of the squad car and on occasions take them to detention.

The officers voiced out of frustration, they would ask in not so nice words, "why don't you spank these girls"? I would explain the situation, "I was stripped of my authority as a parent when my girls made allegations of abuse to Judge Work in Woodward County and were taken from my home. I will never do anything to jeopardize them being able to get away with anything like it again. I will never do anything else to make it possible for them to be taken and placed back in a situation like it again."

I had been duped and set up once, but never again.

I utilized the community resources, agencies I knew were available. Police, Juvenile Affairs, Beaver County District Judge, Beaver County Juvenile District Attorney, Beaver County DHS, Systems of Care, etc., all became involved to help my daughters be restored to responsibility and respect.

It was extremely hard at best. My daughters are worth it.

There was now wisdom and accountability which afforded rest, respectful home environment, and healing.

With these entities closely involved my oldest daughters finally calmed down and settled in. At the very least they realized they were not going to be able to manipulate the legal system in the county we now lived in to get their way. We were finally able to move into my home. The home I had been remodeling in hopes we would all one day live there, all my girls included.

The final custody hearing finally came in Woodward county where the hearings had begun and had kept being delayed for one reason or another. Reports from all the legal entities involved and who had been assisting in the restoration of my children, were submitted to Woodward county.

At this final hearing, I was restored to full parental custody of all three of my girls. Things remained relatively calm with my girls from this point on.

The day my oldest daughter turned 18, January 25, 2013, she moved back to the town where her father lived, finished her final semester of her senior year of high school there in Mooreland, Oklahoma.

Not long after moving in to the house, my husband at the time who had been through the legal custody battle, would stay at his farmhouse on his parent's ranch land seven miles north more and more frequently and stay longer.

One day it seemed warmer than usual as spring was on its way, so I decided to go outside and sit on the front porch. I had been sitting there admiring the sun set no more than five minutes when a patrol vehicle pulled up to the house. He got out of his car walked up to my sidewalk.

On March 15, 2013 Beaver County Sheriff's office served me with divorce papers. I was to sign I received them. Devastated and confused, I slowly went inside, laid down on my bed and cried.

Some of his explanation as to why he wanted a divorce was because God was calling him to preach and in his voiced opinion, I wasn't submissive enough for him. This was wrong to me.

I didn't want a divorce.

I didn't want to face another traumatic loss and event so soon to have just come through such an extreme battle. I did not appear in court. I didn't want anything to do with his decision.

I didn't believe it was God leading him to make this move. I asked him to attend biblical counseling with me. He came to a couple sessions. He walked out of one of the sessions.

I waited and prayed.

I continued in counseling. He quit responding to me completely. He stopped communicating entirely. I waited for seven months to sign the final decree.

With a court date scheduled the following week pending the girls' father's sentencing for the drug charges, he experienced a heart attack.

Ambulance transported him to Woodward Hospital where he was then flighted to Baptist Hospital in Oklahoma City in response to my daughters requesting to do everything possible despite the prognosis offered by the Emergency physician in Woodward.

My daughters and I traveled to the hospital in Oklahoma City. I was there with all three of my daughters standing over him in the Emergency Department. I spoke over him while all his daughters were present and wanted to express their love for him.

I led us in a prayer.

Then the nurses took him to the Intensive Care Unit. As I stood at the foot of his bed in the ICU room watching all the machines keeping him alive, I spoke my peace. In those few moments with a kind of tears I have no words for I released all offense, bitterness, and anger which may have been lingering. August 1, 2013 at Mercy hospital in the ICU the physician pronounced death.

I no longer had to be afraid. I no longer had to fight for my girls. I no longer had to live in fear of a man.

I took my youngest daughters and met my oldest daughter at the funeral home as they wanted to be a part of the funeral plans. I brought all the pictures I had taken, ones which had been returned, and had accumulated over the years of them and their father.

They chose the ones they wanted to include in the slide show as well as the songs playing as the pictures previewed.

Another day, I took my youngest daughters to view their father's body. When we arrived, they had the slide show with the pictures they chose and songs playing. The picture they chose of their father and I's first wedding was removed, however.

It meant there were two versions of the slide show. I asked the lady who worked for the funeral home if she had the first slide show DVD available where I could purchase it for my daughters, since they had chosen it to be included, it was not going to be used, and they were mostly my pictures in the content.

She agreed.

I wrote a check, gave it to the lady, and she in turn gave me the DVD I paid for. Once my daughters had their time viewing their father, we left. Approximately twenty minutes into our drive back home I received a call from the funeral home representative stating they needed the DVD back I had bought. I asked, "Why?"

They explained the niece of the deceased threatened to file charges on them if they didn't get it back, it was their "property". I stated I provided most the pictures and had purchased the DVD. He pleaded they were familiar with this lady and family and they didn't want any trouble. I waited at the nearest gas station for them to come get the DVD.

My mom and I attended the funeral dinner and funeral service together. I was very thankful she was there. I wanted to be there for my girls and as strange as it may seem, I needed the closure. I wasn't allowed to sit with my daughters during the service. His side of family made sure of the sitting arrangements.

The man the girl's father worked for spoke at the funeral as he said he was now a Pastor. His wife was the lady who had the man pick me up from Ft. Worth, put me in the Oklahoma City hotel, and then paid off my fines after I was arrested.

After seven more painful months, I finally arrived at the conclusion and accepted the reality my husband at the time was not going to change his mind. Against what I wanted, I signed and sent in the decree of dissolution of the marriage. On October 29, 2013 the dissolution of the marriage was granted.

I did not appear at the set court hearing but had an attorney who helped with my daughter's court issues appear. I didn't agree with his decision and I didn't want anything to do with the inside of a courtroom.

I continued to grieve with the help of the pastor I was already going to for biblical counseling. I attended every week and then tapered off as I made my way through the pain of loss in a couple years.

The objective, focus, and goals changed from marital discipleship to healing from divorce and the issues the loss triggered within me.

GOVERNOR'S PARDON/ RN: REDEEMED NURSE

Who is a God like you, who pardons sin and forgives the transgression of the remnant of his inheritance? You do not stay angry forever but delight to show mercy. Micah 7:18

In 2008, the ten-year suspended probation sentence was complete. I learned I was now eligible to apply for a pardon. I was directed to the Oklahoma Governor's website where there was a printable application. I printed the paperwork and began working on filling out the information.

Because of the intense battle fighting for my girls from their father, new marriage, moving and then divorce, the pardon submission process took a back burner, as did the writing of this book.

I had just begun both when my life took some intensely painful and challenging turns.

I think there is truth to what some have said, "The enemy will try and distract you as well as he can from gaining ground to victory in and toward God's plans and purposes for your life."

Be it as it may, I did then and do now, continue to perceive and experience even though the painful pruning and vicious valley's life presents us with; God can bring good for His glory.

I don't believe it's over-quoted. I continue to believe this to be true:

Romans 8:28 TP - "So we are convinced that every detail of our lives is continually woven together to fit into God's perfect plan of bringing good into our lives, for we are his lovers who have been called to fulfill his designed purpose."

It took me a little over a year to complete the forms entirely and then about another year to hear of the final decision.

I received a letter from the Pardon and Parole Board August 22, 2012 stating:

"The pardon application you submitted has been forwarded to the Northwest District Community Corrections office due to your address location for the preparation of a Pre-Pardon Investigation. Then said report and application will be returned to this office for further processing."

A Probation and Parole Officer from the Northwest District will contact you during the investigation (on or before October 31, 2012). Please make yourself available to him/her at the earliest available time in order to expedite the Pardon process. The Officer will be the person writing the Pre-Pardon Investigation Report."

I was interviewed by a man from a parole office from the Northwest district and asked questions about my home, finances, etc., who then created a report.

Included in the process was to personally appear before the Pardon and Parole Board in Oklahoma City. I will always cherish the events of the day. They informed me I was able to be accompanied by one other person.

My friend Melissa drove us and sat right next to me before the board which consisted of 6-8 people. She has since gone to be with the Lord. I am forever thankful for her willingness and courage to be by my side during the questioning by the board.

I waited my turn while watching several others sit before the board being questioned and being denied the board's approval for one reason or another.

After watching those go before me, hearing the decisions of their application, it did seem like someone would have to have all their life's affairs in impeccable order and above any sort of scrutiny.

My name was called.

Melissa and I made our way to the front. I sat in a chair beside my brave friend, looking at each member of the board waiting while they all looked down at the paperwork in front of them.

After some time, one man seemed to be the spokesperson and led out in the questioning.

"How long have you been clean and sober?"

I responded, "13 years."

He asked, "How'd you do it"?

There was the question I had prayed for. I had prayed for an opportunity to glorify my Savior and Lord through this process at some point during the day. It was the open door I had longed to walk through and so I did.

I proceeded to share some of my salvation story as they all stared at me. I shared how I'd been called of God by name and surrendered to Jesus in jail. I shared how He delivered me and set me free from addiction, my life has never been the same since.

He thanked me. The other members of the panel smiled and nodded their heads. We left.

After we appeared, the State Pardon and Parole Board sent me a letter in the mail November 21, 2012 stating:

"You were recommended for a pardon by the Pardon and Parole Board during their November 2012 Regular Meeting. The Governor must approve this action for a pardon to be granted. Written notification will be sent to you regarding the final decision."

I'll never forget the day the phone call came from Governor Fallin's office. I answered the call late afternoon February 18, 2013. It was a young lady worked for Governor Fallin. She relayed to me Governor Mary Fallin, just minutes before had approved and signed my full pardon! She went on to explain I would get the certificate with the governor's official seal in the mail. She congratulated me. I thanked her sincerely and profusely.

After the brief conversation, almost before I could get the end call button pressed, I fell to my knees and cried tears of joy and thankfulness to my God and my Savior.

Raising my hands to heaven I thanked Him over and over and over through my tears. He had brought me through. It was a dream and a tremendous need come true!

I received an official letter and copy of the certificate of pardon in the mail dated, March 15, 2013:

"Governor Mary Fallin has granted a pardon to you after a favorable recommendation by the Pardon and Parole Board. A copy of the Certificate of Pardon is enclosed. To obtain a certified copy of the Certificate of Pardon please contact the Secretary of State's office at (number listed). We wish you continued success in the future."

A handful of my closest friends and church family surprised me with what they termed a "Pardon Party!" It is a beautiful thing to have people who support you and celebrate what God has accomplished in your life!

Pardon party my close friends surprised me with after receiving my pardon.

Romans 12:15 TPT
Celebrate with those who celebrate
Romans 12:15 NIV
Rejoice with those who rejoice....

Those of us who have been convicted of crimes and charged with felonies are limited in what type and level of employment we can obtain. It is as if we are still in chains even though we may be released from the physical jail or prison.

The pardon enabled me to obtain an education and license in nursing. I wasted no time. In fact, I had enrolled and was actively attending Certified Nursing classes with my middle daughter, which began December the same year only a month prior to my pardon being granted in 2013.

The instructor allowed me to begin in "good faith" pending the expectation and approval of my pardon. I enjoyed working as a Certified Nursing Assistant (CNA) with a Medication Administration Technician license at a new, near-by assisted living center.

I worked as a CNA for approximately six months then decided to enroll into a Licensed Practical Nurse (LPN) course an hour drive from my home. I completed the enrollment tests and was accepted for the 2013-2014 school year. It was very challenging and very fulfilling.

I leaned on the Lord and relied on Him for my strength as I began LPN school only a week after the funeral of my girls' father. Also, divorce from my new husband was finalized during the year I attended classes.

It's an amazing reality to walk in the resurrection power Jesus won for me at the cross.

I want to continue and become all He says I am.

Philippians 1:6 TPT - "I pray with great faith for you, because I am fully convinced that the One who began this glorious work in you will faithfully continue the process of maturing you and will put his finishing touches to it until the unveiling of our Lord Jesus Christ."

It was an honor to have been asked to sing "Go Light Your World" by Kathy Troccoli at our Pinning Ceremony and to open with prayer at our final graduation.

I'll never forget the humbling honor it was to have shared and been presented with the "Best All Around" award voted by my fellow nursing peers. All the while understanding I am nothing without Jesus. If I achieve anything in this life all glory goes to Him.

Ms. Sharon (lady who led me to Jesus in jail) and Kathy Highfill attending my LPN graduation .

After graduation on June 26, 2014, I completed what they call 'green light', which consisted of an additional thirty-two tests in three weeks.

Even with a pardon I waited another approximately six months for the Oklahoma Board of Nursing to review and investigate my case, due to the previous felony and subsequent charges. The time was lengthened due to long-term illness the woman reviewing it was experiencing. They eventually passed my investigation on to a new person and the process began again. I finally obtained a date and time to appear before the Oklahoma Board of Nursing for a hearing.

On January 13, 2015 I traveled to Oklahoma City for the scheduled Informal Disposition of my case.

I am extremely appreciative for the many prayers going up on my behalf while I worshipped there and back.

I waived a right to an attorney, so I walked into the room alone with a panel of approximately ten people, including the newly appointed Nurse Investigator. All had papers and folders in front of them.

In less than fifteen minutes it was finished. They passed some papers down in front of each person present to sign.

It was a favorable outcome.

I was now eligible to take LPN NCLEX. This is the state test which determines whether I will get an LPN license and be able to practice as a Licensed Practical Nurse in the state of Oklahoma. I scheduled for the test and passed state boards with the minimal 75 questions!

I went on to gain experience working as an LPN in a hospital in rural Oklahoma. I worked nights on a Medical Surgical floor and assisted in the Emergency Department.

I was very thankful to get to the hospital I did and learn from excellent seasoned nurses, especially Jean Bartow, RN, who I completed my leadership rotation with during final semester of the LPN program.

I received great experience at Newman Memorial Hospital in Shattuck, Oklahoma. It prepared me well for the next phase of my nursing education.

After working nights for a year, I felt lead to go ahead and obtain an RN license. I began making the calls to gather the information needed to start the process of requirements and enrollment for a 2016-2017 RN program in Dodge City, Kansas.

If a person had their LPN license and had actively worked for at least one year, as well as having completed the prerequisite course requirements, they were eligible to enter the final year and final semester of the RN program. The school was about ninety miles north from my home.

I had driven approximately an hour one way, 2 hours a day to LPN school the opposite direction. I believed, although difficult, I could manage the drive and it would be worth it.

I filled out a FASFA and received financial assistance and completed the remaining six courses required to enter the final two semesters of a two-year Registered Nurse program.

My grandma Mollie passed away February 13, 2016, only a few months prior to my RN classes beginning. I was praying and began thinking that I may not financially be able to set out on obtaining an RN due to limited finances as a single mom.

My grandma and me

However, my mom called one day and said my grandma Mollie left behind a monetary gift which would now carry us through the year! If it were not for her generosity, I would not have been able to complete the year of classes.

Thank you, Grandma, for showing me grace and believing in me.

Due to taking the ACT so many years earlier (1995) it was suggested I take the COMPASS test on campus to determine my level of academic competency in several areas. The results of the test indicated the classes I could take.

I was eligible to enter directly to the courses I needed. College Algebra and Microbiology, I completed as summer classes. Anatomy, Physiology 2, and Human Growth and Development I completed online. I wrote a paper for and successfully tested out of English Composition.

I also attended a Nursing LPN to RN Transition class on campus prior to officially beginning my final semester of nursing classes. All of it required intense focus and energy.

Before we knew it, it was graduation day! To my absolute delight, all my girls, grandchildren, and my friend Lorene and former Free At Last Ministry assistant had arrived earlier and were in the audience for the morning ceremony.

My family on graduation day!

Later in the afternoon, I was sitting in my graduation robe, in my seat, anticipating my turn to walk across the stage, have my tassel turned to the other side, and receiving my diploma. As I looked up to the left of me in the bleachers there sat my mom!!

Without my knowledge she had come all the way from Oklahoma City to Dodge City, Kansas to be there for my graduation! She had surprised me. What a super, even healing surprise. I stood up in shock and absolute joy, lifted my hands in amazement as if to say, "Wow, look there's my Mom!" at the same time, "Wow, Mom what are you doing here?"

It was a healing moment. It was a moment of redemption. My mom was there in the hospital room telling me I needed help at thirteen years old. All I could think about at the time is going to an institution would prevent me from graduating high school and going to college.

At 42 years old, my mom was there as I was finally completing a college degree.

Picture 1: Wow, there is my mom! Picture 2: Mom came from Oklahoma City to Dodge City, KS to attend my RN graduation.

A little over three years after receiving the governor's pardon, and only a few months prior to entering RN school while attending the summer classes to complete prerequisites, a friend, fellow speaker, and State Representative Sally Kern arranged for a chance to meet and opportunity to thank the Governor for my pardon, in person at the State Capital.

State Representative Sally Kern, Sharon Kennedy, and I at Republican

I was patiently waiting for her when I was told she had arrived. When I stepped around the corner I could hardly believe it. She wore a bright almost neon ORANGE jacket! I gasped first, then literally laughed out loud. She kindly asked why I was laughing. I tried to explain about why I don't wear orange today due to having to wear it in county jail when arrested. Thankfully she grinned and reassured me it represented OSU.

Meeting Governor of Oklahoma, Mary Fallin at the state capital some years after she had signed my full pardon arranged by Representative Sally Kern. She has on a bright orange jacket!

It was a real, redemptive moment with something as silly and seemingly ridiculous as an awful, neon orange suit jacket. It was like God saying, "Yep, I even pardoned you from the county jail orange suits!" Not exactly how I wanted to begin our visit.

The following is the post I made to my Facebook page describing the exciting visit.

Barbara Saunders Livingston
April 6, 2016 ·

Today I was finally able to extend my gratitude to our first female Governor in Oklahoma, Mary Fallin, for approving and signing my full pardon February 18, 2013.

As a public servant who is interested in creating as many jobs as possible for Oklahomans, this one girl here is eternally thankful for the pardon that enables me to hold sufficient employment in order to support my household and family as a single mom. This level of vocation was not possible prior to her signature and seal due to previous felony convictions.

We had a discussion about the devastating rate in which we incarcerate our women in Oklahoma as opposed to reaching and rehabilitating in less oppressive ways. You may be aware that Oklahoma is number one in the nation and world per capita in the number of incarcerated women. This reality was a huge factor and motivation to birth Free At Last Ministries, Inc. in 2005. We operated as a Christ-centered ministry with five denominations on a board and church funding. We sought to disciple women in their transition from jail/prison to stable, sober lifestyles and offer a Christian alternative home environment.

I was able to share with her a bit of my story. My brothers and I being found by child welfare in the basement of a building in Tulsa, Oklahoma to the foster care system and then adoption. I shared briefly the process from institutionalization to addiction to incarceration that ultimately led to my salvation. Jesus then led me into reconciliation with God and biological family through a program that began at the Capital in 1998-99 (the same year I was born-again in a jail cell) called the "Confidential Intermediary Search Program" after being on the "Mutual Consent Voluntary Registry".

Governor Fallin's passion and expressed purpose, not to mention the work and bills she has ushered into law for the best interest of the incarcerated, the struggling souls bound in addiction, as well as, the precious ones in our foster care system is obvious, surprising and quite refreshing to me! I had no idea until I spoke with her the sincerity and extent of efforts she has gone to on behalf of all these people groups!

Governor Fallin shared with me that just this week she passed a law stating the box on a job application that a person convicted of a felony was required to check has to now be removed! I asked her why...what was her motivation for removing that box. She responded, "because it's hard enough to try and change and better one's life without the stigma of always making known the bad decisions of the past" That was my cue to say "HALLELUJAH...PRAISE GOD" ....and you know me, I did!

I spoke with her about a couple other ideas, goals, and dreams I have during our visit, not the least of which was publishing my story and getting it into the hands of ladies in our prisons. To share with them the gospel...the answer and hope of the way out of darkness. As I shared with a young lady this past Sunday in Harper county jail, "There is a way out, but there is only one way out. Jesus".

After meeting, I have a sense of peace knowing God truly ordains our steps and a refreshed resolve to keep fighting the good fight. Ever on my mind still though, are those who are still out there struggling, suffering, and feeling hopeless.

Again, a sincere and very special thank you to Sally Rogers Kern for arranging the morning. I am praying you are feeling better today. I missed you enjoying that moment with us."

I was first pardoned by the King of Kings and Lord of Lords. I've now been pardoned by the Governor of Oklahoma and was offered the unique opportunity to express my gratitude to her in person.

It's a liberating reality!

Ephesians 1:4-8, 11-14 - "For he chose us in him before the creation of the world to be holy and blameless in his sight. In love he predestined us to be adopted as his sons through Jesus Christ, in accordance with his pleasure and will--to the praise of his glorious grace, which he has freely given us in the One he loves. In him we have redemption through his blood, the forgiveness of sins, in accordance with the riches of God's grace that he lavished on us with all wisdom and understanding...."11. In him we were also chosen, having been predestined according to the plan of him who works out everything in conformity with the purpose of his will, in order that we, who were the first to hope in Christ, might be for the praise of his glory. And you also were included in Christ when you heard the word of truth, the gospel of your salvation. Having believed, you were marked in him with a seal, the promised Holy Spirit, who is a deposit guaranteeing our inheritance until the redemption of those who are God's possession--to the praise of his glory.

Half way through RN school, I was friended by a man by the name of Ronald Livingston. We shared some mutual friends on social media and he grew up and graduated high school in the same county I live. I was not looking but after much conversation from a distance, he began pursuing me.

We made an immediate connection. He loves and pursues Jesus with all within him. We met and married months later. I cherish our wedding day. We exchanged our vows and rings, prayed, and most memorable of all we worshipped with family and friends. We had a

Worship Wedding!

The day Ron and I received our marriage license and Our "Worship Wedding"

We now both work at the same hospital. I'm a nurse in ER and Medical Surgical Floor, he works in the Lab and Radiology Department.

The greatest thing about us is we both love, live for, and worship Jesus. He is the kindest, most loving, gentle and giving man I have ever known. He wants, above all things, for others to know the love, grace, and salvation of God. We have this in common.

Thank you, Jesus you continue to write our story. You never leave or give up. Your love is deep and wide and endless. Thank you for another chance.

My girls and I and two grand babies (Ledger and Preston) at home

Thank you for reading my story.

It is my sincere desire and prayer you are edified by my story and in some way, it brings you to a relationship with Christ, if you haven't had one, and a closer relationship if you have felt distant from our Father.

But my story also cries out to the whole world for an opening of our eyes about what is happening to our youth in dysfunctional families, within institutions where they may or may not really understand how to work with traumatized children. One of the most important realities is the gritty, depraved and deadly reality infiltrating our state and all other states. It is important for all who read my story to know this is not something which exists only in the urban areas but is real and close and sometimes taking place in the $1 million home next door to you. It is also playing out right here in Northwest Oklahoma in towns like Clinton, Woodward and even further northwest.

Please take the time to read my wrap up, which includes resources where you may learn more and get help if you find yourself in need of support.

In Christ's Love

Barbara Saunders Livingston

INDEX

Abandonment and Rejection:

A spirit of abandonment and rejection came into my life due to abuse by and relinquishment from my biological parents. It came at such a young age when I was completely defenseless. It created fear and anger which brought about vulnerability to other demonic forces like rebellion and witchcraft. Once those doors are open darkness literally takes over your life.

Drugs, alcohol, and other reality altering chemicals, are doorways to spirits of lust, perversion, insanity, and suicidal suggestions establishing strongholds. Only Jesus' blood, Holy Spirit, and renewing of mind and thoughts by the Word of God can overcome these.

After repentance and salvation, love from the family of God in my church, and as I traveled and shared my story, were and are also powerful healing agents. I would share openly and transparently what I went through and how God rescued, ransomed, and is restoring me. In turn, I was accepted, hugged, loved, prayed for, and supported. I also submitted myself to biblical counseling, discipleship, authority, and direction. These actions slowly demonstrated who God was...real and present....and who He said I was accepted in the beloved.

Adoption:

Adoption is Father God's idea. His family is based on adoption. He has adopted all His children through His Son Jesus. Through the shedding of Christ's blood, I have family. If you are part of God's family, you have been adopted. This truth has changed my identity. Literally, my entire life. I have a Father who will never leave me or forsake me. Hallelujah! If you are in Christ, you are my family.

Jesus said in

John 15:16: You did not choose me, but I chose you and appointed you so that you might go and bear fruit--fruit that will last--and so that whatever you ask in my name the Father will give you.

It is healing to be chosen. I choose you Jesus!

I was given the opportunity to lead seminars on adoption through the Baptist General Convention of Oklahoma during what was known as Women's Weekends and Leadership Training Sweet Spots. There are many adoptees and adoptive parents and families struggling and hurting from the issues which can come with foster care and adoption.

A book I found extremely helpful in identifying some of those ideas by a fellow adoptee Sherrie Eldridge is, "Twenty Things Adopted Kids Wish Their Adopted Parents Knew". With permission I have referred to her book and resources time and time again, as those choosing adoption have approached me with questions and inquiries.

Because adoption can foster abandonment and rejection issues, I have needed to address layer after layer after layer as feelings accompanied by the triggers arise and are uncovered. I did not do this work alone.

Holy Spirit filled, and well-educated people of God walked beside me and worked with me through the most difficult seasons. Thank God there were sensitive, trained, specialized, compassionate people like this put in my journey toward healing.

We were all created with an original intent for love, relationship, family, and bonding with others. When this does not happen or is interrupted by abuse, sin, relinquishment, or ignorance, what can remain is self-hate, anger, depression, and suicidal thoughts. Including any and many variations in between these.

At some point these must be addressed, dealt with, worked through, and delivered and healed. Ultimately it is God's love, Christ's sacrificial blood which brings justice to all situations. His agape love, requiring His perfect sinless life leading to the worst death of all time, evens the scales.

Only Jesus has ever been able to refrain from sin and only Jesus' love is so great to operate with complete selflessness and be willing to lay down their life for another. It is only this kind of love healing the deep, bleeding wounds of a rejected, abandoned, and abused child. Period.

Because of Jesus, I am capable of receiving and giving love today.

I have received exponential healing as I have been open about my story, participated in hours and years of biblical counseling while renewing my mind with the Word of God, and receiving the love and acceptance of the family of God.

Since my salvation there have come about intense seasons of pain by way of divorce, my own choices and decisions of children, loss of loved ones, etc. Painful events usher in grief can be opportunities to explore deeper healing.

I have faced extreme rejection and abandonment triggering deep pain. My chest hurt badly feeling like fire and the tears I cried were like burning acid.

Facing it is key. Facing it soberly.

In those moments I would cry out to Father and say I wanted to come home.

He would reply, "I'm still here. I am the Help you need. I will lead you to the right voice(s) and Holy guidance. What is happening is not who you are".

Rejection is not who I am. Abandonment is not my destiny.

Special recognition and appreciation to a few Pastors, Dr. Tony Barros, Pastor Jerry Hodges (Certified and Specialized in Childhood Trauma), and Robert Huckleberry (Grace Given Ministries) who were equipped and available with the help I needed to walk through and focus on healing through some of those seasons.

As the enemy would come with lies of being unloved, unwanted, given away, abandoned by everyone who was supposed to love me, I was encouraged to talk about, write about, and receive Fathers healing by stating and hearing the truth about who I am and Whom I belong to.

Three papers I was assigned to write and read out loud in my most recent process of biblical counseling, brought tremendous healing are titled, "Honor My Birth", "Baby Barbara", and "God Says, I Believe, About My Birth and Life".

The papers refer to portions of reaffirming scripture: Jeremiah 1:4-5, Ephesians 1:4-6, 11-14, Psalm 139:13-18, Ezekiel 16:4-14.

There was much spiritual warfare in the process. The process was pure obedience and excruciatingly painful. However, it was purifying, powerful, and brought about freedom and peace. You can always be freer if you are willing to walk through the pain transparently and exhibit the humility to request the courage from Holy Spirit to face truth and replace deception and lies with the truth.

It was not a rushed process.

It takes time.

Fear:

I'm so thankful Father walks with me, carries me, loves me through many, many fearful times. His perfect love is actively casting out fear every day.

1 John 4:18 TPT Love never brings fear, for fear is always related to punishment. But love's perfection drives the fear of punishment far from our hearts. Whoever walks constantly afraid of punishment has not reached love's perfection.

My mom shared I had a fear of men since I came to live with them at the time of my adoption at age three.

I lived with a debilitating fear of a man who would kill me or find a way to send me to jail/prison and take my children since I was seventeen years old. The fear died when the man passed away in 2013 a week prior to beginning the Licensed Practical Nursing school. I prayed with all three of my girls for him in the ER and then on the ICU floor, able to say our last words before they pronounced death.

Despite other fears which come and go, Father has brought me further than I ever thought I could go and empowered me to accomplish exceedingly abundantly, and above what I believed I could ever be and do, through faith in Him alone.

I still have moments when I experience fear. However, I do not allow it to stop me from obedience to my Father. He and I work through it together with the Helper and Comforter.

2 Timothy 1:7 TPT For God will never give you the spirit of fear, but the Holy Spirit who gives you mighty power, love, and self-control.

God has also been gracious to lead me to biblical counselors who have helped me through the most difficult, painful times and transitions in my walk. Thank God for those men and women!

Praise Him forever and ever for His patience and power.

IV Drug(s) and Alcohol abuse:

Because of the intravenous drug use I was introduced with and became addicted to, and because I shared needles with others, I contracted two forms of liver disease. I became very sick at the onset at seventeen. The Lord healed me completely of one. Not only healed me but did so in such a way I am completely immune to it now.

The other form I have been in remission from all signs and symptoms since being released from the hospital where I was diagnosed and treated around 1993, 25 years ago.

Only by God's grace did I not die in the car accident when I passed out at the wheel after being up drinking and taking pain pills one night.

I also recovered fully in a hospital from an intentional overdose from a mixture of numerous different pills at sixteen.

I also made it back from a heroin overdose. I fell-out with the syringe in my arm, losing oxygen to my brain. It wasn't until days later when I came-to. It took months to be restored to full functioning mental capacity. I walk in pure grace today with the mind of Christ.

I have been living clean and sober to date for nineteen years. I do not desire nor; must I resist cravings. Jesus completely delivered me. Hallelujah! He answered my prayer for deliverance.

If this was all He ever did for me, it is reason enough to worship Him daily forever.

According to an online site called women's ministry toolbox:

"In 2010, there were an estimated 22.6 million Americans over the age of 12 that were current or former illicit drug users. Since 1980, the number of deaths related to drug overdoses has risen over 540 percent. Over six million children in America live with at least one parent who has a drug addiction."

Homosexuality:

I was unwillingly exposed to homosexual behavior and people who lived this type lifestyle first at 16. There is much confusion, chaos, addiction, and despair which surrounded this environment. I have since met people who believed themselves to be born this way with no way out of the identity and/or compulsion to act out homosexual thoughts, feelings, and suggestions.

As an inmate myself and later speaking in jails and prisons, I've watched first hand this being played out. I present to you God's opinion and thought on the issue below from His holy word. He would not ask of us something which through Jesus and Holy Spirit power we could not overcome and live His way.

His way is best for us. Simply repent, turn to him, and believe and continue to do so. I also know friends and ministers of the gospel who through salvation in Jesus have overcome this evil spirit of homosexuality and are now free.

1 Corinthians 6:9-11 Do you not know that the wicked will not inherit the kingdom of God? Do not be deceived: Neither the sexually immoral nor idolaters nor adulterers nor male prostitutes nor homosexual offenders nor thieves nor the greedy nor drunkards nor slanderers nor swindlers will inherit the kingdom of God. And that is what some of you were. But you were washed, you were sanctified, you were justified in the

224

name of the Lord Jesus Christ and by the Spirit of our God.
Escort   Service/Prostitution/Sex   Slavery   and   Human
Trafficking

Oklahoma Trafficking Safe Line: (800) 522-Safe (7233)

National Trafficking Hotline: 888-3737-888 (TTY: 711) Text
233733 or use the online Live Chat

Between 2012 and 2016 the number of human trafficking cases
logged, and reported calls made has roughly doubled to 7,600 and
26,000, respectively, according to the National Human Trafficking
Hotline.

Modern Day Slavery--Human Trafficking has been defined as a
loss of freedom to another's control by force, fraud, coercion, or to
make an adult engage in commercial exploitation sex acts, or if a
minor, to cause them to commit commercial sex acts. It is the fastest
growing criminal enterprise. Sex Trafficking is just one of many
forms which includes prostitution and escort services.

The encounter, when I met the two men decades older than me
when I was seventeen, is minimal in comparison to many stories I've
learned the details of and been educated about, while seeking training
and raising awareness of sex trafficking in Oklahoma. Nevertheless,
any form of sexual exploitation of a minor for selfish, personal,
financial gain or profit is illegal, immoral, and grossly heinous.

The definition of fraud according to Webster's Dictionary is

1. **a)** Deceit, trickery; specifically: intentional perversion of truth in order to induce another to

    part with something of value or to surrender a legal right.

    b) and act of deceiving or misrepresenting: **TRICK.**

2. **a)** a person who is not what he or she

    pretends to be: **IMPOSTER.**   One who defrauds: **CHEAT**.

    b) one that is not what it seems or is represented to be.

The men in my story both presented themselves as business men and the situation I walked into as being a "job interview". They explained I would be performing a certain skill of dealing cards.

This was intentionally fraudulent.

I learned later, when it was too late, they both engaged in and had an extensive involvement and history in what was termed to me later as purchasing escorts and prostitutes for their own dates and sexual services.

These "services" were in exchange for food, clothing, money, a place to live, and drugs. They both knowingly set the stage for and turned the situation into entrapment where I sensed obligation and preyed upon my existing vulnerabilities in the situation.

The older man was thirty-nine years older than me (56 years old). The younger of the two was 24 years older (43 years old). I was still a minor at the time.

Even though I had been through so much by this time, this setup brought on a whole new level of shame, fear, oppression, and bondage. They knew what they were doing and had done it before. I did not.

I was the victim.

I didn't realize I was a victim until many years later, unfortunately. Today, I am no longer a victim. I am free in Christ. I know who I am. I know Who I belong to, Jesus. I have been blood-bought, sanctified, and sealed forever.

Marrying the younger man and having three children with him turned the situation into my "norm". I had learned to adapt and survive from a very young age. To just not feel, shut down emotionally, or do enough drugs to escape, or take on a tough personality as a front to handle what I was facing and the shame-filled situations.

I became used to the stares and second looks from others. I became accustomed to, as best as one can, being asked if he was my father and if he was my daughters grandpa.

I was actively serving on a women's state leadership team with the women's office for the Baptist General Convention of Oklahoma when I was then asked to be a part of a human trafficking task force which consisted of attending a Human Trafficking Conference.

There were two ladies sharing their stories at the conference. As the two ladies shared their stories, true/false statements were presented to me as well as general facts about sex trafficking. I began to get a clearer picture of what happened to me at seventeen.

I was sharing briefly about the time with the two men as though I was an escort, or it was a fancy way of saying prostitution. Now I was being educated it was a form of Modern Day Slavery, sexual slavery.

During this same time, September 2010, I was invited to sit for a recorded interview with Channel 9 News regarding this portion of my story. You can view the segment at http://m.news9.com/story.aspx?story=13226868&catId=112032#

I began attending training courses designed to educate and prepare to raise awareness about the issue of modern day slavery and human sex trafficking. One appointment I was called on to speak and share some of my story with a room full of District Attorneys, Judges, and other legal representatives in Clinton, Oklahoma. As I shared the portion of my story entailed of the two men having me at 17 living with them in a condo right there in Clinton, their own town, I could hear gasps and statements of shock and looks of concern.

Without a doubt, the level of awareness was raised for those in attendance. For me, it was yet another redemptive healing moment. It's as if Father God has sent me on a healing tour. Opening doors for me to share my story in the exact places and leading me to the very people, families, or entities associated with the deepest parts of my pain, poor choices, and violations. In doing so, it brings with it a holy justice and a God ordained vindication of sorts. God orchestrates these appointments in such a way there leaves no room for the enemy, or anyone else who would doubt it is His work, in my life, bringing me to a place of truth, on-going transformation, and total   restoration.

"The FBI reports that in the United States, the number of children, usually girls, who are forced to do someone's sexual bidding is well over 100,000. The age range is nine to nineteen. The average age is just eleven years old.

It is also big business. Worldwide, the sex trade generates an estimated $32 billion in income each year. It is second behind only the drug industry as the world's leading criminal enterprise. It is what the FBI calls an epidemic.

Sex trafficking isn't just going on "out there" somewhere. It's happening in your state. Maybe even your town." (The White Umbrella Campaign, 2012)

Recent laws have passed, address the issue this way:

'A measure to better protect youth from human trafficking was signed into law in 2012. House Bill 2518, by Rep. Sally Kern and Sen. Josh Brecheen, strengthens Oklahoma's human trafficking laws in the hopes of deterring the industry in the state.'

"Oklahoma's high rate of poverty, incarceration, domestic abuse, teen pregnancy and drug addiction makes it easy for traffickers to find vulnerable women and children in our state, but we need to strengthen our laws to protect these unsuspecting victims," said Brecheen, R-Coalgate. "The 13th Amendment to the Constitution prohibits slavery, and we must do all we can to prevent modern day slavery in our local communities, and this bill will help with that effort."

HB 2518 modifies the definition of "human trafficking for commercial sex" to include the recruiting, enticing, harboring, maintaining, transporting, providing, purchasing or obtaining, by any means, a minor for purposes of engaging the minor in a commercial sex act.

"These victims could be your neighbor's children or even your own children. Oklahoma citizens need to be educated and informed that human trafficking is a very real and present danger in our state," said Kern. "With this new law, our state has taken an important step in protecting our state's youth. We want these predators to know that we will not tolerate this crime in our communities."

Currently, under Oklahoma law if a minor consents to go along with a sex trafficking recruiter then the recruiter is provided some legal protection. Under HB 2518, consent of a minor cannot be used as a defense in court.

Another major change is, currently, sex traffickers can only be penalized if they recruit through fraud, deception or coercion. Under the new law, anyone found recruiting for sex trafficking, regardless of how they do it, will be penalized.

"Victims of sex trafficking come from big cities and small towns. They come from affluent, middle class and low-income families and from many ethnic backgrounds," said Brecheen. "We need to educate ourselves, our children and our neighbors about the dangers of this growing epidemic and protect our communities."

HB 2518 went into effect November 1, 2012.

For more information, contact:

Sen. Brecheen: (405) 521-5586

Rep. Sally Kern: Facebook

America is now considered to be the #1 destination for child sex trafficking. (State Department of Justice Statistics, 2008)

Oklahoma cities are on human trafficking routes (I-35, I-40, I-44) throughout the Midwest and beyond, and Oklahoma and six bordering states have already passed laws targeting human trafficking.

According to the Department of Justice the average age of a prostitute is now 14, average entry age 12-13. 78% of prostitutes say they did not initially choose it, 84% have been homeless at one point, and 80-90% report childhood sexual abuse history. 70% report childhood incest, 75% have attempted suicide, and 92% of prostitutes surveyed they want out immediately.

90% of prostituted women have a pimp or trafficker, minors are still being arrested as child prostitutes, less than 2% of the customers are ever arrested.

An estimated 5 million photos and videos of children circulate the internet each day. The majority of child porn is prepubescent, 20% of Internet porn is child porn, 6% are infants or toddlers--(preverbal), 99% of viewers are men, 91% white, case studies--70% of men convicted of sexually abusing minors also view child porn, less than 1% are ever rescued.

In 2011 Utah Attorney General says law enforcement officers collected enough images of child porn and images of child sexual abuse if they were stacked one on top of the other, they would rise nearly 2000 miles high.

According to cdc.org victims include all races, ethnicities, sexual orientations, gender identities, citizens, non-citizens, and income levels. Victims are trapped and controlled through assault, threats, false promises, perceived sense of protection, isolation, shaming, and debt. And, victims do not have to be physically transported between locations to be victimized.

Perpetrators of sex trafficking often target people who are poor, vulnerable, living in an unsafe situation, or searching for a better life. For example, youth with a history of abuse and neglect or who are homeless are more likely to be exploited.

The vulnerable are targeted: inner-city children, single parent homes, low income/poverty/low education, runaways and throwaways, children growing up in alcohol and drug addictive family systems or cultures, illegal or undocumented foreign nationals, troubled teens, unhappy or insecure, minors--groomed online social networks.

What is being done?

Trafficking Victims Protection Act (TVPA) of 2000

Trafficking Victims Protection Reauthorization Act of 2003 (TVPRA)

Prosecutorial Remedies and Other Tools to End the Exploitation of Children Today Act of 2003 (PROTECT)

Trafficking Victims Protection Reauthorization Act of 2008 (TVPRA of 2008)

The Customs and Facilitations and Trade Enforcement Act (2009)

Trafficking Victims Protection Reauthorization Act of 2013 (TVPRA of 2013)

National Defense Authorization Act of 2013

The Racketeering Influenced Corrupt Organizations Act (RICO)

The Mann Act of 1910, amended in 1978 and again in 1986

Oklahoma's first law in place 2008

Oklahoma City task force started in 2009

Law enforcement training began in 2010

Tulsa, Oklahoma Task Force started in 2010

Internet Safety Program

First Safe House for victims in Oklahoma City

Safe Houses nationally

Abortion:

1 Timothy 1:15-16 TPT I can testify that the Word is true and deserves to be received by all, for Jesus Christ came into the world to bring sinners back to life—even me, the worst sinner of all! Yet I was captured by grace, so that Jesus Christ could display through me the outpouring of his Spirit as a pattern to be seen for all those who would believe in him for eternal life.

While lost in darkness I underwent a total of four abortion procedures.

I was not aware God calls abortion murder at the time of these procedures.

I did not understand God knew us in our mother's womb, has the hairs on our head numbered, has a plan for us before the foundation of the world.

All I knew is I was in scary desperate situations at these times. It seemed better for my baby, to take their life than to bring them into the hopeless circumstances I found myself in.

Adoption was not an option either due to having been adopted myself and going through what I was.

After my salvation, I learned the Father calls abortion murder. Murder is sin.

I learned because of Jesus shedding His blood on the cross in my place, all my past, present, future sins are forgiven. I learned also the Father not only wanted me forgiven but also healed.

The Holy Spirit led me to some online pictures, descriptions, and videos. These described in vivid detail what takes place during abortion procedures. As I viewed the pictures including the instruments used I slid to the floor.

During those moments I began to understand the grievousness of what I had submitted to.

My heart broke.

I knelt there crying, confessing, and repenting. Crying out to God to forgive me.

I didn't deserve His grace.

Holy Spirit reminded me of Jesus' blood, how it is sufficient for even these heinous acts.

Father not only invited me to be forgiven but His desire is for me to also be healed.

In the course of the following week with the help of my Pastor, I walked through the healing process. The process began with my eyes being opened to the truth. Literally seeing my sin for what it was as the images of what I had done were before me and led to brokenness and repentance.

From confession of what had taken place to another person, I was invited to receive forgiveness and grace through Jesus. Up until this point I had not seen the abortions as representing real babies. It was an act of survival for me and a way out of a horrible life for them. I had been deceived.

After this step I was invited to name my children.

This was very difficult.

I prayed as I worked through the grief. Father's presence was very close and loving during this process. There was not a hint of condemnation, judgement, or shame in my pastor's approach, attitude, wording, or demeanor.

By God's mercy and leading, I named my four children. I named them after the new identify of their mother.

Chosen, Justified, Redeemed, and Princess are whole, healed, and in the presence of God today.

They are free. So am I.

About a week after the confession, repentance, and healing, I received an invitation to speak at a Pregnancy Center benefit banquet.

They were specifically holding this event to raise money to purchase an ultrasound machine allowing the mothers who come in for pregnancy tests and test positive to see their baby in the womb.

The hope and potential is when a mother sees her baby is real and can view it in her womb, the probability of her choosing abortion decreases significantly.

God did not waste any time after my healing process to share His forgiveness and grace.

During the event in Durant, Oklahoma at the Bryan county Pregnancy Center Benefit Banquet, I shared my story, how through Jesus, God not only forgives but heals.

There were thousands of dollars raised in the evening towards a machine where through images could help prevent moms from having to go through and see the images of murder I saw so many years later. Babies lives can be saved.

2 Corinthians 5:19-21 (TPT) In other words, it was through the Anointed One that God was shepherding the world, not even keeping records of their transgressions, and he has entrusted to us the ministry of opening the door of reconciliation to God. We are ambassadors of the Anointed One who carry the message of Christ to the world, as though God were tenderly pleading with them directly through our lips. So, we tenderly plead with you on Christ's behalf, "Turn back to God and be reconciled to him." For God made the only one who did not know sin to become sin for us, so that we who did not know righteousness might become the righteousness of God through our union with him.

A MESSAGE FROM THE AUTHOR

In 2008, God led me to begin writing this book of my story, His life-transforming power in my life. In 2018, ten years later, it is finally complete!

Father God continues to restore my life. He has taken all my pain and poor decisions and now utilizes my life; the good, the bad, the ugly for His glory to help others know Him. It is all I really desire now. I want my life to point to Him, serve Him, and go wherever He leads.

Through the mercy of God and in His timing, He provided me with pieces of the puzzle of my life which gave me peace and led to purpose. I can now present my story giving Him glory for my hope and salvation.

Psalm 71:7 TPT It was you who supported me
from the day I was born, loving me, helping me
through my life's journey. You've made me into a
miracle; no wonder I trust you and praise you
forever! Many marvel at my success, but I know it is
all because of you, my mighty protector.

There have been many powerful moments and experiences the Lord has led me into by His grace. Too many to mention. His love, provision, and power have taken my breath away over and over again.

What I would consider my "worst" day in Christ is still infinitely and eternally more beautiful, better, and blessed than what I would have considered my "best" day lost in darkness, confusion, and addiction.

I enjoy His presence and our relationship. He walks with me through each day. I hear His voice. He will never leave me or forsake me. I trust Him. I love, adore, and worship Him!

He is Good. He is Deliverer. He is Protector. He is Defender. He is Father. He is Husband. He is Friend. He is the Lifter of my Head. He is Sustainer. He is All In All.

He is at the right hand of the Father ready and willing to prove Himself to be who He says He is in your life.

Will you repent and receive Jesus today?

HE RESCUES. HE RANSOMS. HE RESTORES.

Father in Heaven, I recognize I am lost. I repent, turn away from sin right now. I receive you Jesus into my life. I desire you to be Lord and Leader of every part of my life. Thank you for dying in my place and rising from the dead so I might enjoy forgiveness, healing, and new life in you. Guide me to my purpose by Your power and authority. Give me the words to share with others who You are and what You can do. Let Your Love and Light shine through me always. I am Yours and You are mine for the remainder of my days into forever.

In Jesus Name, Amen.

References

1. Mary Frances Bowley, "The White Umbrella: walking with survivors of sex trafficking", Moody Publishers, 2012.

2. Don Besig, "Flying Free", Copyright 1979, Shawnee Press, Inc., Delaware Water Gap, PA 18327

3. M. Scott Peck, MD, "The Road Less Traveled", Simon and Schuster Publishing, 1978.

4. Sherrie Eldridge, "Twenty Things Adopted Kids Wish Their Adopted Parents Knew", Penguin Random House, 1999.

5. U.S. Department of Health and Human Services, Substance Abuse and Mental Health Services Administration. (2013). Moral Reconation Therapy. National Registry of Evidence-based Programs and Practices. nrcpfc.org

6. Beth Moore, "Breaking Free: Making Liberty in Christ a Reality in Life", LifeWay Press, 1999.

7. Beth Moore, "Believing God", LifeWay Press, 2004.

8. Center for Disease Control and Prevention, National Human Trafficking Resource Center. cdc.gov

9. Dennis Rainey and Dave Doehi, "The Best Gift You Can Ever Give Your Parents", Familylife, 2004.

10. Department of Justice, Human and Sex Trafficking Statistics, 2008

11. Polaris Project: Freedom Happens Now, Washington D.C., polarisproject.org

12. Rusty Surette, "Woman Shares Story of Teen Years as Sex Trafficking Victim", News9, 2010.

    http://m.news9.com/story.aspx?story=13226868&catId=112032#

ENDORSEMENTS

"I heard Barbara's story almost 15 years ago and have watched how the Lord has taken her through peaks and valleys, joys and disappointments. She's the real deal and doesn't mind letting you know that Jesus is the real deal and is still in the business of redeeming our past and using our story for His glory. You will be encouraged by her story, but you will also be challenged to share your faith with others."

Kelly King
Women's Ministry Specialist
LifeWay Church Resources
One LifeWay Plaza
Nashville, TN 37234-0147
Office: 615.251.2810
kelly.king@lifeway.com
www. lifeway.com/women
twitter and instagram: @kellydking

"I had the opportunity of being Barbara Saunders' Pastor when she first came to know the Lord. Her transformation from darkness to light was a true joy to behold! Her testimony both then and now has been a source of grace and strength to all who know her story. God has brought her a long way in her Christian journey. It has been a blessing to me personally to see how the Lord is using her life."

Dr. Russell Duck, Pastor
First Baptist Church
Elk City, Oklahoma

Barbara is real and unashamed of the work of God in her life. She was once a slave, but our Redeemer set her free! Her life is proof our God still works miracles! It was a joy to be her pastor and to witness firsthand the blessing of God on her life.

Tim and Glenette Russell
Tim presently serves as Director of
Missions of Grady Baptist Association located in Chickasha, Oklahoma.

It is for freedom that Christ has set us free. Stand firm, then, and do not let yourselves be burdened again by a yoke of slavery. Galatians 5:1. That Scripture adequately sums up the life of Barbara Saunders Livingston. I have had the privilege of knowing Barbara for eighteen years.

My youngest daughter Lana had met she and her children in our local homeless shelter and we became acquainted at that time. As a retired teacher, counselor in rehabilitation and prison ministries, I have seen very few individuals truly break free from the bondage of addiction. Barbara is one of those individuals whose life was miraculously and deeply touched by God Almighty and set free.

Her convictions, dedication of service to helping "the lost" is without question! Her travels to various venues around the United States to give her heartfelt testimony is truly a work of the Holy Spirit and is truly anointed!

As this book is the story of her life, it is also the heartfelt cry to "the lost" and hurting people in the world of addictions, heartache, and pain. I truly believe that it will be anointed and bring "lost souls" into the Kingdom of God through our Lord and Savior, JESUS CHRIST.

Respectfully in Faith, Hope, and Love,

Free At Last Ministries Administrative Assistant
Lorene Witt

241

I have known Barbara almost sixteen years. I have always been encouraged and blessed how she is always ready and willing to testify for Christ. How He has brought her through, 'the good, the bad, and even the ugly' of her past to the present. She is a real example of how God can use every bit of our lives to grow, change, and live for Christ.

An excellent read for any woman.

Sharon Kennedy
Free At Last Ministry
Woodward, Oklahoma

This book is truly an inspiration. Barbara's story is proof, and a living testimony, that through Jesus Christ we certainly can do "all" things. Her accomplishments, and the major obstacles she overcame in achieving them, speak for themselves. She also tells a sobering truth that society has either turned a blind eye to, or is ignorant of the fact, that human trafficking is a multi-billion-dollar industry that goes on every day in our towns and cities. She knows, she was a victim! This is truly a must read—

Dennis Hall Senior Pastor
The Recovery Church, Duncan Oklahoma
Prison and Jail Chaplain

Sometimes on this journey called "Life" someone comes along that awakens the hope that is planted in each human heart. This is where Barbara steps into my life.

In the summer of 2010, I was handed a copy of Barbara's short story and told, "I needed to read this testimony!" Barbara's story was full of transparency, recovery, and most of all hope, for all those who suffer at the hands of addiction, mental illness and abuse of every kind.

I pray that each person who reads this book will open their heart and let the hope of Jesus Christ explode... and your faith be strengthened, knowing that you too can arise out of the ashes of your past and shine into a dark world. This book will challenge you as you examine your own heart and ask yourself, "if you have the courage and faith to reveal the dark secrets of your own life, to tell people about Christ, no matter what?"

I know this story of Barbara's personal life will affect the lives of the people she loves very much, and I want to thank them also for their support and encouragement of her as she reveals the unfolding of Christ in her.

May God richly bless each person reading this book as they walk their own personal journey of life, overcoming their own past... With the small, seed of hope, speaking in a still, small voice, "If she can do it, so can I."

Deborah Hall B. Msc.
The Recovery Church, Associate Pastor
Spiritual Teacher and Mentor at, "PAM" Positive Attitude Ministry
Prison & Jail Chaplain

Barbara was adopted into our family when she was just over two and a half years old. After only a few weeks of assimilating into the family routine she seemed to adjust well. She had an older sibling and less than two years later a younger one. She was an average child, in an average family, doing what average families do.

Just prior to becoming a teenager, Barbara was literally seized by evil and dark forces! She spent many years in this state, which caused pain and anguish both to herself and those around her.

Thanks be to God and her willingness to accept His salvation, He pulled her out of her bondage just as fast as she was pulled into the evil realm. Through many struggles and painful reconciliation, she, through God's strength found what she needed to overcome the physical, emotional and legal problems she faced due to her years of living in this terrifying, sinful and immoral state.

It has taken her years to come to the point where she has not only overcome her past, but through her faith, trust and obedience claimed her victory through Jesus Christ!

Barbara is dedicated to fulfilling God's purposes in her life. She believes that one purpose is to share her story with others facing similar-seemingly insurmountable obstacles. She wants others who believe their past can only negatively affect their future to know that through God's free gift of love and grace they too can be set free and that God will provide what is needed for them to fulfill their purposes.

LaVonne Kiser, Mom
Retired Kindergarten Teacher

ACKNOWLEDGEMENTS

Special thank you to my husband Ronald Livingston whose energy and servant heart is the motivation I needed to see this book to completion. Your passion for our Savior and the Word of God strengthens me. Your sweet consistent love and encouragement is healing.

Tremendous appreciation to Rachael Van Horn and Sarah Nishimuta for all the editing hours you both contributed. Your writing and creative perspective is a true gift. The suggestions you made added to the integrity and expertise of the book. You both made the process exciting and a joy!

A colossal thank you to my youngest daughter Brook, who even though in her sophomore year of high school herself, was patient and understanding as I spent an immense amount of time studying and working on homework to obtain an RN license. To all my girls, thank you for forgiveness and grace. I love you with all my heart.

Overwhelming heartfelt and immense gratitude for all the people and families who make up First Baptist Church Woodward for teaching me the Word of God and demonstrating His love in exceptional ways. You accepted me as a new believer, brought me up in my faith, and believed in me, by providing countless opportunities to exercise spiritual gifts, including leadership. Especially Janice Brown who helped to edit, print, and fold the thousands copies of my testimony pamphlet and have them ready for distribution at events.

Shout out to Lana Witt Fugh for friending this homeless girl who had just stepped out of a jail cell.

Monumental recognition to Lorene Witt, who served as an assistant and ministry partner. The hours she put in with transportation, meetings, and child care as I traveled to speak, as well as offering her administrative and organizational skills, were invaluable to the ministry. Most of all her faithful friendship and mother-like conversation, prayers, and sacrifices over the years are recognized and appreciated. I smile sometimes when I consider who God puts together for His purposes.

A special word of thank you goes to my grandma Mollie, who passed away February 13, 2016, only a few months prior to my RN classes beginning. If it were not for her generosity, I would not have been able to complete the year of classes. Thank you, Grandma, for showing me generous grace and believing in me.

Special thank you to Rita with Beaver county juvenile affairs, Abby Cash Beaver county Juvenile District Attorney, Beaver county District Judge Reddick, and to Judy and Shanna with Harper County Systems of Care. These utilized their legal positions to take the time, listen, and made the wise decisions proved to be in the best interest of my children.

Gratitude to my friend Ashley, who I carpooled with to and from our RN classes. You made the road time such a joy. You are one of the smartest, kindest people I've ever known. I'll never forget your gentle touch as you laid your hand on me and prayed for me one day in the car. Through the year of extreme ice and fires; we did it! With God's help; we did it!

Extraordinary honor to those whom I encountered along the way who expressed care and concern. Those who demonstrated the love of God to me when at my worst. Those who took the risk to reach out, to step out of their comfort and safe space to show some kindness and grace and touch my brokenness. Anyone who exhibited courage, vocalizing the Word of God, praying, and great faith speaking the name of Jesus into my life, I honor you.

Utmost respect to those who faithfully, diligently live what they preach and teach. I would not be where I am today without the men and women of God, the Father put in my life.

ABOUT THE AUTHOR

Barbara Saunders Livingston is a gifted author, speaker, and advocate who uses her gripping story to demonstrate the power of God's deliverance and love. Barbara has served on various women's leadership teams including a human trafficking task force for the Baptist General Convention of Oklahoma educating and raising awareness. She has shared her life-transforming testimony, for nearly two decades, across the United States including prison events hosted by the Billy Graham Foundation; Gideon's State and International Conferences. Barbara has appeared on American Family Radio, Living Proof Radio Show, and as an awards presenter aired on GAC. She has written contributing articles for Nashville's Power Source Music Magazine and Pearls Women's newsletter.

Barbara is a Registered Nurse. She and her husband Ronald, have a blended family with six children, five grandchildren, and reside in Northwest Oklahoma.

Barbara's hope for this book to provide copies to women incarcerated, homeless shelters, recovery homes. If you would like to contribute and sow into this ministry for books, you can contribute here at http://paypal.me/Restored2cor517.

If you would like to engage her for a speaking engagement, ministering, sharing her story, you can contact her at restored2cor517@yahoo.com. You can visit her website at abbaloves.us. Follow her on social media:
Facebook Page- Rescued, Ransomed Restored
Instagram-rescued,ransomed.restored
Twitter- @Barbara77857156